D0778996

Three Argu.
Against Whole Language &
WHY THEY ARE WRONG

Three Arguments Against Whole Language & WHY THEY ARE WRONG

STEPHEN D. KRASHEN

HEINEMANN
Portsmouth, NH

Heinemann
A division of Reed Elsevier Inc.
361 Hanover Street
Portsmouth, NH 03801–3912
http://www.heinemann.com

Offices and agents throughout the world

Library of Congress Cataloging-in-Publication Data
Krashen, Stephen D.
      Three arguments against whole language & why they are wrong /
   Stephen D. Krashen.
         p.   cm.
      Includes bibliographical references and index.
      ISBN 0-325-00119-7 (alk. paper)
      1. Reading—Language experience approach.   2. Literacy.
   I. Title.
   LB1050.35.K73   1999
   372.41'6—dc21   98-45123
                                                                      CIP

Editor: Lois Bridges
Production: Elizabeth Valway
Cover design: Catherine Hawkes, Cat and Mouse
Manufacturing: Louise Richardson

Printed in the United States of America on acid-free paper

03 02 01 00 99 DA 1 2 3 4 5

Contents

Introduction

The first three chapters in this collection respond to the most frequently cited arguments against whole language. Chapter One, "Eye Fixation Studies Do Not Disprove the Goodman-Smith Hypothesis," reviews studies in which subjects' eye movements are recorded as they are reading. The claim has been made that these studies provide firm scientific evidence that readers examine text "completely," examining the text in great detail. This chapter expands on a point made by Frank Smith (1994): Subjects in these studies have little choice but to read in great detail because of the bizarre and unnatural experimental situation they are placed in. This paper was previously published in the *Claremont Reading Conference Yearbook, 1997*.

Chapter Two, "Does Context Interfere with Learning to Read?" deals with the second popular argument against whole language. Whole language claims that context helps children learn to read because it helps readers make more accurate predictions (i.e., it makes texts more comprehensible). Critics maintain that context (e.g., pictures) actually interferes with learning to read because it diverts attention from the text. I argue that this only occurs when context is too rich, or "overdetermining." Critics also claim that readers only appeal to context when they are unable to do fully accurate reading of individual words, and that poor readers need to do more of it. Once again I argue that the experimental situation dictates this kind of strategy: Subjects are focused on reading individual words accurately and quickly, and better readers, of course, will be better at this and thus have less need for context, a point also noted by Frank Smith.

Chapter Three, "When Whole Language Means Real Reading, It Is a Consistent Winner over Skills in Method Comparison Studies," deals with the third argument against whole language, method comparison studies. The claim has been made that in these studies, "skill-building approaches" have been shown to be superior. I argue that this is not the case: When whole language is defined correctly, it is a consistent winner. While the arguments in Chapter One and Chapter Two do not help us decide between the comprehension hypothesis and competing hypothesis, the data presented in Chapter Three is firmly on the side of the comprehension hypothesis.

The next section discusses the "real solution" (McQuillan 1998). Chapter Four, "Eliminating Print Deprivation," presents the incredibly simple solution to problems in literacy: access to books. Providing access to good reading material is not even the last alternative these days—it is not even on the drawing board. There is, however, overwhelming evidence that it works. (A version of part of this chapter was published in *Educational Leadership,* volume 55, 1997–1998, with the title "Bridging Inequity with Books.")

The final chapter considers the logical consequence of early intervention with a skills-based approach. "Phonemic Awareness (PA) Training for Prelinguistic Children: Do We Need Prenatal PA?" is a reaction to the frantic drive for early intervention and the failure to see that grade-level standards are arbitrary. (I offered a copy of this chapter to a member of the California Reading Task Force, asking her if she would like to see my paper on "prenatal phonemic awareness development." She said that it "sounded like a good idea.") This chapter was previously published in *Reading Improvement.*

References

McQuillan, J. 1998. *The Literacy Crisis: False Claims and Real Solutions.* Portsmouth, NH: Heinemann.

Smith, F. 1994. *Understanding Reading.* 5th ed. Hillsdale, NJ: Erlbaum.

1

Eye Fixation Studies Do Not Disprove the Goodman-Smith Hypothesis

Trying to pinpoint meaning by studying where the eyes fixate can be like trying to study digestion by analyzing knife and fork movements.

—FRANK SMITH, *UNDERSTANDING READING*

The Goodman-Smith view of literacy development hypothesizes that literacy development and comprehension are closely related (Goodman 1982; Smith 1994), in agreement with the Input Hypothesis (Krashen 1985). Figure 1–1 illustrates the Goodman-Smith hypothesis. Before readers encounter a piece of text, they have made predictions about what they are about to read. These predictions come from their knowledge of the world, what they have read so far, and their knowledge of language, which can include knowledge of sound-spelling correspondences. They then look at the text to see if it matches what they have predicted. If the match is "close enough," the text is "understood." In other words, their prediction has been confirmed. A crucial aspect of this

1

Figure 1–1

The Goodman-Smith Hypothesis for Reading Comprehension

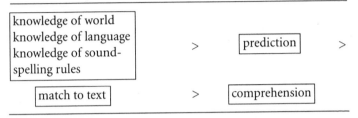

view is that readers do not have to notice every detail of the text; they only have to confirm that it is the predicted text. It is also important to note that the model does not predict that readers will be able to guess the next word of any text they happen to be reading; rather, their knowledge of the world, the text, and language helps them reduce the alternatives, which relieves them of the burden of having to note every detail of the text.

Language acquisition and literacy development can occur when the reader encounters new aspects of language in the text that he or she has not yet acquired but is developmentally "ready" to acquire; this could be new sound-spelling correspondences, new vocabulary, or new grammar.

One of the oft-repeated arguments against this view and in favor of "skill-building" approaches are reports that readers "completely sample the visual array" (Stanovich 1986), that they do not engage "in the wholesale skipping of words, nor are they markedly reducing their sampling of visual features from the words fixated" (368). This finding appears to contradict the view that fluent readers make predictions and utilize text only to confirm these predictions.

I expand here on a point already made by Smith (1994, 87): Studies showing complete sampling of text are studies in which eye movements are monitored while subjects read. What is crucial is that in these studies, subjects are put in a situation in which intensive, detailed reading is necessary: No other strategy is possible. In eye-fixation studies, one or more of the following conditions is present:

1. In all eye-fixation studies, texts are selected by the experimenter, with no consideration of readers' interests. Many of the studies, in fact, do not even use coherent texts; subjects read individual words and sentences (e.g., Rayner and Morris 1992). When texts that are more coherent are used, they are typically irrelevant to the reader and are sometimes quite difficult.

    In Just and Carpenter (1980), for example, college students read texts selected from *Time* and *Newsweek* on scientific discoveries, technical inventions, and biological mechanisms. Just and Carpenter point out that most students were not familiar with the information contained in the passages. Here is an excerpt from one passage:

    > Flywheels are one the oldest mechanical devices known to man. Every internal combustion engine contains a small flywheel that converts the jerky motion of the pistons into the smooth flow of energy that powers the drive shaft. The greater the mass of a fly-wheel and the faster it spins, the more energy can be stored in it. But its maximum spinning speed is limited by the strength of the material it is made from. (334)

    Unless you are really interested in mechanics, the eyes don't move much. In fact, they glaze over.

    Just and Carpenter (1987) point out that their readers fixated nearly as frequently (77 percent of the content words) on a "less technical" article from *Reader's Digest*. This less technical article "described the expeditions of John Colter, an early nineteenth-century explorer who traveled through the American West" (431–432), a passage I suspect would be of great interest to a minority of readers.

Just and Carpenter (1980) conclude from their studies that in "ordinary" reading, "almost all content words are fixated" (329), noting that this applies to narratives as well as scientific texts. They also, however, note the following:

> Of course, this is not the case when adults are given simple texts, such as children's stories; under such circumstances, these same studies show an increase to an average of two words per fixation. (330)

In other words, as reading is made less demanding, eye fixation behavior becomes more normal.

2. In all eye-fixation studies, readers are asked comprehension questions or are asked to summarize the passages after they read them; they must try to remember what they read as they read it, which is certainly abnormal behavior. This is true in all eye-fixation studies I have read.

    Subjects in Just and Carpenter (1980) were told not to "memorize," but they knew they would be asked to orally summarize the passages after they read them. In addition, they were asked "not to reread the passage or parts of it" (335). It is thus no surprise that the readers fixated on more than 80 percent of the content words in the passage.

    In Ehrlich and Rayner (1981), comprehension questions were asked either before or after reading the passage, and subjects were told that "the most important part of the experiment was to be able to answer the questions" (644). In Rayner et al. (1991), subjects were asked to read five- to eight-word sentences and then "report the sentence verbatim (or paraphrase it, although subjects tended to report the sentence verbatim)" (168). After the subject reported as much of the sentence as possible, "the experimenter recorded the subject's response and gave feedback by reciting the stimulus sentence" (168). This is strong encouragement to read carefully.[1]

3. In eye-fixation studies, readers are placed in an awkward physical position for reading, making it harder to focus on the text and meaning. As Smith (1994) has noted, in some studies subjects cannot even move their heads, because of chin rests, bite plates, or helmets (255). In addition, quite often texts are read off computer screens that allow subjects to see only one line at a time. Making the situation even more artificial, in some studies, before reading the text, readers

> must look at an asterisk located in the upper–left hand corner of the screen (where the first word will eventually appear) and at the same time press a "ready" button. If the reader's point of regard is not within one degree of the fixation point, then the text is not displayed, and the experimenter must recalibrate. If the accuracy is adequate, then the text appears on the screen and remains there until the reader indicates that he or she has finished reading by pressing a "done" button. Then the fixation point reappears and the subject initiates presentation of the next screen as just described. (Just and Carpenter 1984, 153)[2]

To summarize: In eye fixation studies, readers are asked to read something they did not select and that may be either bland or boring but is surely irrelevant to the reader; readers are placed in a Clockwork Orange–type contraption while reading; the text is presented on a computer screen; and readers are told they have to try to remember what they are reading as they are reading it. In addition, they are sometimes told that there might be odd spelling errors in the text but they should ignore them (e.g., Zola 1984). It is hard to imagine a stranger situation.

Rayner and Pollatsek (1987) feel that "these concerns are ill founded," noting that Tinker (1939) showed that "reading rate and comprehension of subjects in a soft easy chair with a book did not differ from the reading rate obtained in the eye-movement laboratory" (24). It is true that Tinker's subjects had equal performance in rate and comprehension when reading in front of the camera and when reading without the camera. Subjects in the "normal condition" were not, however, in an easy chair, as Rayner and Pollatsek claim; rather, they were reading "at a table" (Tinker 1939, 742). In all conditions, Tinker's subjects read passages that were not self-selected (paragraphs from the Chapman-Cook Speed of Reading test), and comprehension questions were asked. Thus, Tinker only showed that photographing eye movements did not significantly alter reading speed and comprehension on tests of reading comprehension, a situation in which most people would read intensively, focusing on details. Eye-fixation studies do not tell us about fixations during ordinary reading of self-selected material that readers are interested in reading, without comprehension testing.

Despite the fact that conditions in eye-fixation studies force careful reading, the results are surprisingly consistent with the hypothesis-testing view. Ehrlich and Rayner (1981) and Zola (1984) reported that when subjects read words that were highly predictable from context, fixation duration was reduced. Ehrlich and Rayner feel, however, that their results do not support the hypothesis-testing position because in their view the hypothesis-testing position predicts no fixation at all for very predictable words; partial information from the parafovea should be enough. The hypothesis-testing view does not necessary predict zero fixation in these cases. Rather, the reader needs to note enough of the word to confirm what it is. With more predictable text, this fixation will be less thorough and take less time, but not necessarily zero time. And this is what the research shows.

Zola (1984) reported that his subjects fixated longer on words with small spelling errors, even when the words were highly predictable from context, a result that appears to conflict with the view that readers use minimum visual information. As in other studies, however, the conditions promoted very careful reading. Even so, as noted above, Zola's subjects fixated a shorter time on predictable words, which is consistent with the hypothesis-testing position.

Additional evidence that readers do not focus on every detail comes from Rayner et al. (1991). In this study, readers read text through a window that only allowed them to see a few letters at a time. Rayner et al. reported that "reading performance (rate) improved with increasing window size" (170). When the window only allowed a few letters, reading was "difficult but not impossible" (170). This result suggests that it is not necessary or desirable to focus on every letter.

Speed Readers: An Alternative Interpretation

Just, Carpenter, and Masson (1982; cited in Just and Carpenter 1987) compared fixations of normal and "speed" readers. My interpretation of their results is that dense fixations are not "normal." Just, Carpenter, and Masson reported that non–speed readers fixated on 77 percent of the content words (readers of the Colter passage from *Reader's Digest*), while speed readers only fixated on 40 percent of the content words. As usual, comprehension tests were administered, making the entire situation unnatural. Just et al. reported that normal and speed readers produced summaries of the passage of equal quality. The normal readers, however, did better on a reading comprehension test. Just et al. conclude that "the summaries are imprecise indicators of comprehension" (Just and

Carpenter 1987, 447). In my view, the summaries are more valid than the reading comprehension test: Just, Carpenter, and Masson's results actually show that speed readers do perfectly well in reading for their own purposes, but do not do especially well when reading according to someone else's agenda.

Notes

1. Brady and Moats (1998) argue that just the opposite is true, that "asking participants about the content of what they read is a realistic way to assess if they were reading normally" (9). But when readers know in advance that they will be quizzed on the content of what they are reading, or know that they will have to paraphrase what they are reading, the process is not normal: Instead of focusing on understanding the message (the route to long-term memory), readers in this condition will try to put information in short-term memory while they are reading—they will make a deliberate effort to remember, a process that disrupts comprehension (Smith 1998).

2. Brady and Moats note that this kind of situation "is not the way someone would like to sit to read for pleasure" but ask whether there is any theoretical rationale "that holding one's head still and reading off a monitor alters the cognitive requirements of reading" (9). Of course there is: Head movements are a natural part of reading, as is allowing the reader to focus on what he or she wants to focus on. Restricting subjects' gazes so they must read what and where someone else tells them to read is violating what is perhaps the most central aspect of normal reading.

References

Brady, S., and L. Moats. 1998. "Buy Books, Teach Reading." *The California Reader* 31 (4): 4–10.

Ehrlich, S., and K. Rayner. 1981. "Contextual Effects on Word Perception and Eye Movements During Reading." *Journal of Verbal Learning and Verbal Behavior* 20: 641–655.

Goodman, K. 1982. *Language, Literacy, and Learning*. London: Routledge Kegan Paul.

Just, M., and P. Carpenter. 1980. "A Theory of Reading: From Eye Fixations to Comprehension." *Psychological Review* 87: 329–354.

———. 1984. "Using Eye Fixations to Study Reading Comprehension." In *New Methods in Reading Comprehension Research*, ed. D. Coors and M. Just, 151–182. Hillsdale, NJ: Erlbaum.

———. 1987. *The Psychology of Reading and Language Comprehension*. Newton, MA: Allyn and Bacon.

Krashen, S. 1985. *The Input Hypothesis*. Beverly Hills: Laredo.

Rayner, K., A. Inhoff, R. Morrison, M. Slowiaczek, and J. Bertera. 1991. "Masking of Foveal and Parafoveal Vision During Eye Fixations in Reading." *Journal of Experimental Psychology: Human Perception and Performance* 7: 167–179.

Rayner, K., and R. Morris. 1992. "Eye Movement Control in Reading: Evidence Against Semantic Preprocessing." *Journal of Experimental Psychology* 18: 163–172.

Rayner, K., and A. Pollatsek. 1987. *The Psychology of Reading*. Englewood Cliffs, NJ: Prentice Hall.

Smith, F. 1994. *Understanding Reading*. 5th ed. Hillsdale, NJ: Erlbaum.

———. 1998. *The Book of Learning and Forgetting*. New York: Teachers College Press.

Stanovich, K. 1986. "Matthew Effects in Reading: Some Consequences of Individual Differences in the Acquisition of Literacy." *Reading Research Quarterly* 21: 360–407.

Tinker, M. 1939. "Reliability and Validity of Eye-Movement Measures of Reading." *Journal of Experimental Psychology* 19: 732–746.

Zola, D. 1984. "Redundancy and Word Perception During Reading." *Perception and Psychophysics* 36: 277–284.

2

Does Context Interfere with Learning to Read?

I n this chapter, I argue that the results of studies of the impact of context are consistent with the Comprehension Hypothesis, the hypothesis that we acquire language (Krashen 1985) and develop literacy (Goodman 1982; Smith 1994) by comprehending messages.

Comprehension of messages is necessary, but is not sufficient, for language and literacy development. Figure 1–1 reviews the Goodman-Smith model of the comprehension-acquisition process as applied to reading. Before readers encounter a piece of text, they have made predictions about what they are about to read. These predictions come from their knowledge of the world, what they have read so far, and their knowledge of language, which can include knowledge of sound-spelling correspondences. They then look at the text to see if it matches what they have predicted. If the match is "close enough," the text is "understood." In other words, their prediction has been confirmed. Language acquisition can occur when the reader encounters new aspects of language in the text that he or she has not yet acquired but is developmentally "ready" to acquire; this could be new sound-spelling correspondences, new vocabulary, or new grammar.

Figure 1–1
The Goodman-Smith Hypothesis for Reading Comprehension

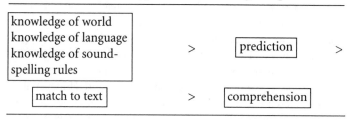

A crucial aspect of this model is that readers do not have to notice every detail of the text; they only have to confirm that it is the predicted text. It is also important to note that the model does not predict that readers will be able to guess the next word of any text they happen to be reading with 100 percent accuracy; rather, their knowledge of the world, the text, and language helps them reduce the alternatives, which relieves them of the burden of having to note every detail of the text.

In the Goodman-Smith model, the "use of context" means the use of anything other than the item the reader is currently examining to predict what that item is. It could be background, non-linguistic knowledge, knowledge of grammar, and knowledge of sound-spelling correspondences. It is reasonable to hypothesize that good readers will be able to make greater use of context—that is, they will be able to make more accurate predictions—because they know more about the world, have larger vocabularies, have acquired more grammar, and have more competence in sound-spelling rules, all a result of reading (Smith 1994). Goodman (1982) states this as follows: "Skill in reading involves not greater precision but more accurate first guesses based on better sampling techniques, greater control over language structure, broadened experiences and increased cognitive development" (39).

Guess Every Word?

It is sometimes maintained that because readers cannot always guess the next word in a text they are reading with full accuracy, the prediction model must be incorrect. This kind of attack goes back a long way: Flesch (1955) told parents that "guessing . . . is a bad habit that stands in the way of your child's ever learning to read properly" (99). Citing Gough, Alford, and Holley-Wilcox (1981), Flesch (1981) noted that readers can "only" guess about one word in four while reading. While other studies have reported better rates of prediction, even with little context provided, one word in four with full accuracy is an astounding result.[1] Such high accuracy confirms that because of context, readers are able to reduce the possibilities enormously.

Context thus limits the possibilities but does not reduce them to one possibility in every case. The finding that readers can predict what the next word is going to be even only 20 percent of the time is strong evidence that much of the work of determining the next word has already been done before the reader gets there.

The Effects of Context

Context effects can be categorized as follows:

1. *Overdetermining.* When context is very rich, it is possible that the language acquirer will pay no attention to the oral or written message that accompanies it. In terms of the Goodman-Smith model, predictions will be made from the situation that are very specific, and no help from the text is required.

    Very few of us, for example, bother to read the fine print that accompanies the bag of peanuts one gets on airplanes, unless one has a special interest in the fat content. The context (expectations of what we get to eat on planes), the size of the bag, and when it is delivered is usually more than enough context to make a very accurate prediction of what is in the bag.

2. *Underdetermining.* Sometimes context provides no help at all and the hearer or reader is completely dependent on the linguistic features of the input. This occurs frequently in school, and in experimental situations.

3. *Partly determining.* In this situation, context helps the acquirer reduce the possibilities of what is being heard or read, it but does not reduce them to certainty. The acquirer must still examine the print or pay attention to the aural input. This kind of context is common in everyday life. We look at print all the time, even though context provides us some help. Location tells us where the milk is in the supermarket, and our knowledge of milk containers helps us narrow our decision, but these days we need to at least glance at the label to see if we are getting regular, low-fat, or nonfat milk.

   The Comprehension Hypothesis predicts that language and literacy development will only take place when context is partly determining and when the input contains items that the acquirer has not yet acquired but is ready to acquire. Thus, both overdeterming and partly determining context are helpful for comprehension, but only partly determining context helps acquisition.

4. *Deceptive.* In these cases, context leads us to the wrong conclusions. An argument against the use of context to enhance language and literacy development is the claim that many contexts are useless or deceptive. This occurs occasionally, but most contexts are helpful. Beck, McKeown, and McCaslin

(1983) found that 61 percent of the contexts they examined in basal readers were of help in acquiring new vocabulary, providing at least some clues to meanings of unfamiliar words ("partly determining"), while 31 percent were of no help, and only 8 percent were "misdirective." Deceptive contexts are fairly rare in everyday life. As Smith (1994, 16) points out, we are rarely surprised.

Schatz and Baldwin (1986) concluded that most of the contexts they examined were not helpful for vocabulary acquisition. Context in their study, however, extended only to three sentences. Arriving at the meaning of new words may take more than this. Consider the following example:

> He takes out an envelope from a drawer, and takes paper money from it. He looks at it ruefully, and then with decision puts it into his pocket, with decision takes down his hat. Then dressed, with indecision looks out the window to the house of Mrs. Lithebe, and shakes his head. (443)

From this passage, it would be hard to arrive at much of the meaning of *ruefully,* but with wider context (the entire book) and deeper understanding of the character and what has happened in the story, readers would have a much better chance to add something to their knowledge of this word. Schatz and Baldwin really demonstrated that it is possible to prevent vocabulary acquisition by restricting contexts to an unnatural degree.

The Effects of Pictures on Learning to Read

It has been argued that context, in the form of pictures, actually interferes with learning to read: Samuels (1967) concluded that "pictures function as distracting stimuli in that they [draw] attention away from the printed words" (340). In this section, I examine this argument.

Samuels presented kindergarten children with words printed on index cards in one of three conditions: (1) no picture—the word appeared alone on the card; (2) a simple picture condition in which the word was accompanied by a drawing portraying the object represented by the word; and (3) a complex picture condition in which the word was accompanied by "a colorful picture which had been cut out of a reading primer" (338). In "learning trials," children were shown the words in one of these three conditions. If the child was unable to read the word, the experimenter supplied it. "Test trials" alternated with learning trials. No feedback was given on test trials and pictures were not included. As shown in Table 2–1, those in the no-picture group had the lowest score in the acquisition trials but did the best on the test trials. The two picture groups achieved similar scores, doing well on the acquisition trials but significantly worse than the no-picture group on the test trials. Samuels suggests that the presence of pictures can interfere with learning how to read.

Singer, Samuels, and Spiroff (1973–1974) extended Samuels' results. First- and second-grade children read words in one of

Table 2–1

The Effect of Pictures on Reading Single Words

TREATMENT	ACQUISITION TRIAL	TEST TRIAL
No picture	25.3	19.2
Simple picture	39.4	11.3
Complex picture	36.9	11.6

Source: Samuels (1967)

four conditions: (1) word-picture, similar to the picture conditions in Samuels (1967); (2) word-no picture, similar to the no-picture condition in Samuels (1967); (3) sentence-picture, in which the word was accompanied both by a picture as well as a sentence using the word (e.g., for the word *cat,* the sentence was "The cat sleeps"); (4) sentence-no picture, which consisted of the target words, the sentences used in condition 3, and no picture. The target words were written in an artificial alphabet.

As in Samuels (1967), subjects participated in "study trials" (learning trials) and test trials with no cues. As shown in Table 2–2, the group with the least contextual support, word-no picture, did the best on the test trials, while the group with the most support (sentence-picture) did the worst: The difference between the word-no picture condition and the other conditions was statistically significant, but none of the other differences were. Similar results were obtained for an analysis of the number of trials needed to get all four target words correct.

Harzem, Lee, and Miles (1976) presented twenty six-year-old children with words that they previously could not read under one of four conditions, with five children participating in each

Table 2–2
The Effect of Pictures and Sentence
Context on Reading Single Words

	MEAN
Word-no picture	34.98
Word-picture	28.43
Sentence-no picture	26.23
Sentence-picture	23.29

Source: Singer, Samuels, and Spiroff (1973–1974)

condition: (1) appropriate picture—the picture corresponded to the word presented (e.g., a picture of some stairs accompanied by the word *stairs*); (2) an inappropriate picture—the picture did not correspond to the word presented; (3) a "nonsense" picture not resembling any object; and (4) no picture. Words were presented to the children representing all four conditions in mixed order in two ways: as "acquisition trials," in which children saw each word twice and were told the correct pronunciation of the word when they made a mistake or made no response; and as a test, in which no feedback was given.

Harzem, Lee, and Miles reported that children in the appropriate picture condition did the best in the acquisition trials but did not do the best in the test trials, both in tests given right away (Table 2–3) and twenty-eight days later. (The study used both massed and distributed conditions; this data is from their massed condition.)

The study is important in that it shows that the problem is not pictures per se; rather, it is the relationship of the picture to the text. They conclude that "what is to be avoided is a direct equivalence between the picture and the printed text, especially in the case of the presentation of single words" (322).

Table 2–3
Effect of Appropriate and Inappropriate
Pictures on Reading Single Words

CONDITION	ACQUISITION TRIALS	TEST
Appropriate	37.4	24.4
Inappropriate	28.9	25.9
Nonsense	24.3	19.3
No picture	27.1	29.4

Source: Harzem, Lee, and Miles (1976)

The results of all three studies can be easily interpreted in terms of the previous discussion: The picture conditions in Samuels (1967), the picture and sentence conditions in Singer, Samuels, and Spiroff (1973–1974), and the "appropriate picture" condition in Harzem, Lee, and Miles (1976) did not lead to better acquisition because the context was overdetermining. Children in the underdetermining conditions (no picture) were forced to attend to the print more and had the advantage of hearing the word pronounced more frequently while they were doing so. Deceptive context (inappropriate picture in Harzem, Lee, and Miles) was no more damaging than overdetermining context: In both cases, the children attended less to the print.

These studies do not, however, provide clear evidence that words are best taught in isolation, without pictures: The condition hypothesized to be best for language acquisition—partially determining context—was not included in any of the three studies.

The Effect of Real-World Context on Learning to Read

It has been argued that real-world context is actually irrelevant in learning to read. The fact that very young children can read print in the environment is not considered "real reading" but is a "pseudo-stage" that precedes real reading. This argument appears to be supported by Masonheimer, Drum, and Ehri (1984), who tested two- to five-year-olds who had received no alphabetic instruction on their ability to read environmental print. Their sample consisted of children who could "read" eight out of ten samples of environmental print in context (e.g., the McDonald's sign with the restaurant pictured and with the golden arches in the background). When some of the helpful context was removed (the golden arches appeared without the picture of the restaurant), performance declined, and when no context was provided, "performance dropped dramatically" (257). Children were also not proficient at detecting changes in the print when context was missing.

The explanation provided in the previous section applies to this situation as well. The examples of environment print used in this study were all overdetermining (others included Jack in the Box, Pepsi, Star Wars, Coke, and Kmart). As this study notes "there is no 'press' on the subject to look beyond the cues that are easiest to discern and most obvious ... from a functional point of view, no purpose is served by attending to letters" (269). Masonheimer, Drum, and Ehri conclude that from their findings, "we know that environmental print experiences are not responsible for [progress in reading]" (269). Their results, in my view, only show that some environmental print experiences are not responsible for progress in reading: those that are overdetermining. Their results are thus not counterevidence to the hypothesis that we learn to read by understanding text, with the aid of predictions made by context. (A similar interpretation applies to Stahl and Murray [1993], as McQuillan [1998] points out.)

Vukelich (1994) demonstrates what can happen when overdetermining context is made partly determining. Kindergarten children were compared in three conditions for a fifteen-week treatment: normal play; play that contained natural, meaningful print (e.g., a SALE sign in a play store); and play with print in which an adult facilitated comprehension of the print in a way that was appropriate to the play (e.g., pointing to the SALE sign and asking the child, "Are these the shoes that are on sale?"). Children were tested on their ability to read the words out of context and in context three weeks after the treatment ended. For out-of-context reading, the most stringent test, those who had adult interaction recognized the most words, followed by those with print without interaction, followed by the control group. The group with adult interaction was able to read about three out of ten words at the end of the treatment, which appears to be modest; it suggests a substantial long-term gain, however, for a child in a print-rich environment with adult interaction.

Do Good Readers Use Less Context?

Many studies have been published that appear to show that good readers make less use of context, a result that suggests that context is something only poor readers appeal to when they need it. West and Stanovich (1978) was one of the first, and many subsequent studies have used similar designs with similar results (e.g., Allington and Strange 1977; Allington 1978; Stanovich and West 1979; Perfetti, Goldman, and Hogaboam 1979; Schwantes, Boesl, and Ritz 1980; Schwantes 1981; West et al. 1983; Leu, DeGroff, and Simons 1996, and many others). In West and Stanovich (1978), fourth graders, sixth graders, and adults (college students) were asked to read simple sentences aloud, as quickly as possible. Sentences contained target words in one of the three contexts:

1. "congruous" (e.g., The dog ran after the cat)
2. "incongruous" (e.g., The girl sat on the cat)
3. no context (e.g., the cat)

Subjects first saw the context and then, after a delay of one half of a second, the target word. Analysis of reaction times revealed that for the younger subjects, the fourth and sixth graders, there was "contextual facilitation"—that is, they read the target word more quickly when the context was congruous, and read the target word more slowly when the context was incongruous, or deceptive. For adults, however, there was no difference between the no context and incongruous context conditions, suggesting that "better readers . . . make less use of context" (721).

The usual interpretation of this data is that when we read, we first do not appeal to context; rather, we attempt to read the word in isolation and appeal to context only when this fails. Under this interpretation, West and Stanovich's results show that poor readers need more context to supplement their lower ability to read words in isolation. Good readers, however, do not need to appeal to context.

These studies, however, are not inconsistent with the Goodman-Smith model. In the experimental situations used in context studies, subjects are heavily focused on form, on reading a target word aloud quickly and accurately. In some of the studies, the context is presented on paper while the target word is on a screen, and, as noted, there is a half-second interval between the presentation of the context and the target word. Better readers in these studies will appear to utilize less context simply because they are better at reading words in isolation (Perfetti and Hogaboam 1975), a fact that is very consistent with the Goodman-Smith model. They developed this ability from real reading. This higher level of ability to read words in isolation allows them to ignore context, helpful or deceptive. Children who have trouble reading words in isolation, in "contrived or instructional situations are forced to use context as much as they can since phonics won't work for them" (Smith 1994, 282).

If put in a situation in which the emphasis is on rapid and accurate reading of the word *cat*, readers of this book will read the target word *cat* in the previous examples quite rapidly in all three contexts. Our excellent ability to read words in isolation results in minimal interference from the incongruous context in sentence 2 and we have little need of the friendly context in sentence 1.

West and Stanovich (1978) was one of the first studies to claim that context use was associated with poor reading. Leu, De-Groff, and Simons (1996) is one of the most recent. First graders read a "predictable text" with nine words substituted for the original words. The new target words were syntactically and semantically consistent with the sentence but were not consistent with the text as a whole. Children read the story orally and were then asked to tell what they remembered about the story. Readings of the nine target words were classified as "discourse appropriate" (the original word) or "graphically expected" (the new target word). The study reported that better readers had more graphically expected responses. Thus, poor readers appeared to be influenced more by the overall context. In addition, poorer readers appeared to profit more from helpful context: They read the first half of the story more slowly than the good readers, but read the second half just as quickly.

The explanation for the 1978 results also works in 1996: In Leu, DeGroff, and Simons, as in West and Stanovich, subjects were reading orally in a test situation and were thus focused on correctness. Good readers have better competence in reading words in this kind of condition and are thus less affected by context. The study does not tell us how the ability to do accurate, rapid reading aloud of individual words develops.

Conclusion

Studies of context are often cited as showing that "top-down" theories of reading are not correct. My goal in this chapter was to show that studies of context are consistent with the Goodman-Smith position. Thus, studies of the use of context do not help us decide between competing theories of reading development.

Note

1. Aborn, Rubenstein, and Sterling 1959 reported a 47% rate with sentences of eleven words and 38% in six-word sentences, with 24% of nouns and 37% of verbs guessed correctly overall.

References

Aborn, M., H. Rubenstein, and T. Sterling. 1959. "Sources of Contextual Constraint upon Words in Sentences." *Journal of Experimental Psychology* 57: 171–180.

Allington, R. 1978. "Effects of Contextual Constraints upon Rate and Accuracy." *Perceptual and Motor Skills* 46: 1318.

Allington, R., and M. Strange. 1977. "Effects of Grapheme Substitution in Connected Text upon Reading Behavior." *Visible Language* 11: 285–287.

Beck, I., M. McKeown, and E. McCaslin. 1983. "Vocabulary Development: Not All Contexts Are Created Equal." *Elementary School Journal* 83: 177–181.

Flesch, R. 1955. *Why Johnny Can't Read.* New York: Harper and Row.

———. 1981. *Why Johnny Still Can't Read.* New York: Harper and Row.

Goodman, K. 1982. *Language and Literacy: The Selected Writings of Kenneth S. Goodman.* Boston: Rutledge and Kegan Paul.

Gough, P., J. Alford, and P. Holley-Wilcox. 1981. "Words and Context." In *Perception of Print: Reading Research in Experimental Psychology,* ed. O. J. L. Tzeng and H. Singer, 85–102. Hillsdale, NJ: Erlbaum.

Harzem, P., I. Lee, and T. Miles. 1976. "The Effects of Pictures on Learning to Read." *British Journal of Educational Psychology* 46: 318–322.

Krashen, S. 1985. *The Input Hypothesis.* Beverly Hills: Laredo.

Leu, D., L. DeGroff, and H. Simons. 1996. "Predictable Texts and Interactive-Compensatory Hypotheses: Evaluating Individual Differences in Reading Ability, Context Use, and Comprehension." *Journal of Educational Psychology* 78: 347–352.

McQuillan, J. 1998. *The Literacy Crisis: False Claims and Real Solutions.* Portsmouth, NH: Heinemann.

Masonheimer, P., P. Drum, and L. Ehri. 1984. "Does Environmental Print Identification Lead Children into Word Reading?" *Journal of Reading Behavior* 16: 257–271.

Perfetti, C., S. Goldman, and T. Hogaboam. 1979. "Reading Skill and the Identification of Words in Discourse Context." *Memory and Cognition,* 7, 273–82.

Perfetti, C., and T. Hogabaum. 1975. "Relationship Between Single Word Decoding and Reading Comprehension Skill." *Journal of Educational Psychology* 67: 461–469.

Samuels, S. 1967. "Attentional Processes in Reading: The Effect of Pictures on the Acquisition of Reading Responses." *Journal of Educational Psychology* 58: 337–342.

Schatz, E., and R. S. Baldwin. 1986. "Context Clues are Unreliable Predictors of Word Meanings." *Reading Research Quarterly* 20: 439–453.

Schwantes, F. 1981. "Effect of Story Context on Children's Ongoing Word Recognition." *Journal of Reading Behavior* 13: 305–310.

Schwantes, R., S. Boesl, and E. Ritz. 1980. "Children's Use of Context in Word Recognition: A Psycholinguistic Guessing Game." *Child Development* 48: 612–616.

Singer, H., S. Samuels, and J. Spiroff. 1973–1974. "The Effect of Pictures and Contextual Conditions on Learning Responses to Printed Words." *Reading Research Quarterly* 9: 555–567.

Smith, F. 1994. *Understanding Reading.* 5th ed. Hillsdale, NJ: Erlbaum.

Stahl, S., and B. Murray. 1993. "Environmental Print, Phonemic Awareness, Letter Recognition, and Word Recognition." In *Examining Central Issues in Literacy Research, Theory, and Practice,* Forty-Second Yearbook of the National Reading Conference, ed. D. Leu, C. Kinzer, L. Ayre, J. Peter, and S. Bennett, 227–233. Chicago: National Reading Conference.

Stanovich, K., and M. West. 1979. "Mechanisms of Sentence Context Effects in Reading: Automatic Activation and Conscious Attention." *Memory and Cognition* 7: 77–85.

Vukelich, C. 1994. "Effects of Play Interventions on Young Children's Reading of Environmental Print." *Early Childhood Research Quarterly* 9: 153–170.

West, R., and K. Stanovich. 1978. "Automatic Contextual Facilitation in Readers of Three Ages." *Child Development* 49: 717–727.

West, R., K. Stanovich, D. Feeman, and A. Cunningham. 1983. "The Effect of Sentence Context on Word Recognition in Second- and Sixth-Graders." *Reading Research Quarterly* 19: 6–58.

3
___

When Whole Language Means Real Reading, It Is a Consistent Winner over Skills in Method Comparison Studies

"Whole Language"

The term "whole language" has been used many ways. In this chapter, I will use it to refer to application of the "comprehension hypothesis" to early literacy. The comprehension hypothesis claims that we acquire language (Krashen 1985) and develop literacy (Goodman 1982; Smith 1994) through comprehension of messages. The core of whole language is providing children with interesting texts and helping them understand these texts. "Whole language" is sometimes used to refer to practices that are just the opposite, such as giving children incomprehensible texts. It is also used to refer to methods in which children memorize large numbers of sight words, unlike the use of this term here.

A popular argument against "whole language" is that method comparison studies have shown that skill-building methods are superior. I argue here that when whole language is defined as providing comprehensible texts, it is a consistent winner in these studies.

In other publications, I have reviewed studies that investigate the effectiveness of reading interesting texts among older acquirers (Krashen 1993; Mason and Krashen 1997; see also Elley 1991). There is no question that reading is superior to skill-building approaches in these studies, as long as the treatments last long enough.

In this chapter, I review studies dealing with younger acquirers, mostly first and second graders. In these studies, classes in which reading is emphasized are compared with classes in which less reading is done. The reading classes are usually labeled "whole language," but not always.

In addition, I review studies in which methods are labeled "whole language," but were not. As Stahl (1994) has noted, children in classes labeled "whole language" do not necessarily do more real reading than children in "traditional" or "basal" classes. We will see that in these cases, they do not do as well.[1]

Whole Language as Real Reading

The review that follows combines the traditional literature review with a "vote-getting" review. Meta-analysis was not performed because of the lack of suitable data in some cases, and because too few studies were included that used the same dependent variable. Nevertheless, the results are quite consistent.

In several studies, observations and measurements confirm that the students did a considerable amount of meaningful reading. In others, the classes are described as "literature-based" and/or researchers indicate that a great deal of real reading was included.

McKenna et al. (1995) found no difference in attitude

toward reading between children in classes labeled "whole language" and "traditional" in two studies. In a third study, they did detailed observations of two first-grade "whole language" classes. Although both were labeled "whole language," there was a clear difference between the classes with respect to print: In one class, far more print was on display and books were more accessible to the students. Reading attitudes were significantly higher in this class.

In Merver and Hiebert (1989), second graders in a "literature-based" program clearly read more than children in a "skills-based" program (see Table 3–1). Standard deviations for the skill-based group were zero because all reading was assigned; there was no variability in the amount read.

While the skills-based children were questioned on everything they read, the literature-based children "talked and wrote only about a small portion" of what they read (535). Merver and Hiebert did not probe reading achievement but reported that children in the literature-based program spent significantly more time selecting books in the school library and had more sophisticated selection strategies; all literature-based children sampled the

Table 3–1
Reading Done in School (Total Words in One Week)

| | LITERATURE-BASED ($N = 10$) | | SKILLS-BASED ($N = 10$) |
	Mean	SD	Mean
High-achieving students	22,731	8,180	6,805
Low-achieving students	8,344	3,237	4,643

Source: Merver and Hiebert (1989)

text of the books they were interested in, but nine of the ten skills-based children looked only at the cover. Literature-based children also tended to read more at home, but the difference was not statistically significant for the one week they were studied.

Hagerty, Hiebert, and Owens (1989) compared second, fourth, and sixth graders who did a "literature-based" program with comparison students who had a traditional "skills-based" program. The former included reading tradebooks and writing on topics chosen by the students, while the latter consisted of teacher-directed instruction and "filling out teacher-assigned worksheets which provided practice on particular skills or reading assigned textbook passages" (455). Some free reading was allowed. The students in the literature-based classes outperformed those in the skill-based classes on a standardized test of reading comprehension, and on a writing sample judged on organization, sentence structure, usage, capitalization, punctuation, spelling, and format.

In Morrow, O'Connor, and Smith (1990), "at-risk" kindergarten children received an extra sixty minutes per day of either traditional instruction that focused on learning the alphabet (with some storybook reading) or a literature-based program that focused on storybook reading (teachers reading to the children), recreational reading, and "literature activities" for one academic year. The experimental class excelled on reading comprehension and story retelling tests, as well as on a test of "concepts about books and print." On traditional standardized tests focusing on skills and reading readiness, there were no significant differences between the groups.

Eldredge (1991) compared first graders in "whole language" classes in which "most of the classroom time was spent in recreational and functional reading and writing activities" (32) with basal/skills-based classes. The whole language group also had fifteen minutes per day of phonics in isolation. Of course, the skills/basal group also had instruction in phonics. The whole language group was significantly better on all measures after one school year (Table 3–2), including performance on tests of phonics and reading attitude. Eldredge's results are consistent with the comprehension hypothesis, the hypothesis that it is comprehensible input—in this case real reading—that causes literacy development, but it could also be claimed that skills played a role: The whole language group's phonics sessions included sound segmentation and blending activities, while the skills/basal group had instruction only on basic sound-symbol relationships.

Klesius, Griffith, and Zielonka (1991) found no difference between whole language and traditional first-grade student gains on a variety of measures, including a test of phonemic awareness. They note that "independent reading was encouraged" in the whole language classes, but it is unclear just how much comprehensible input the two treatments had. What is clear is that the whole language group made gains equal to that of the comparison group in "skills" (phonemic awareness, spelling) as well as reading comprehension, with much less "skill building" done in the class.

Morrow (1992, 1996) compared second graders in a literature-based program with children from a basal-type program over one school year. Both groups included children who were considered

Table 3–2
Comparison of Whole Language and Basal Group; Mean Scores

GROUP	N	VOCAB.	RC	PHONICS	ATTITUDE
Whole language	56	36.5 (7.1)	33.4 (6.3)	63.0 (12.2)	79.5 (19.3)
Basal/skills	49	32.1 (8.8)	27.1 (8.8)	57.6 (12.5)	71.6 (20.4)
Effect size (d)		.55	.82	.43	.40

standard deviations in parentheses

Source: Eldredge (1991)

middle class as well as "disadvantaged" children. Experimental and comparison groups devoted the same amount of time to reading instruction (7.5 hours per week), but the experimentals' reading time was spent differently: Children were read to daily; teachers engaged them in at least three "literacy activities" per week (e.g., children retelling and rewriting stories, book sharing, keeping track of what they had read); and children had at least three sessions per week in a comfortable "literacy center" for 30 minutes at a time. Literacy center activities included reading, writing, performing stories, binding books, and so on. Experimental students spent about 3.5 hours per week with basals and 4 hours with literature. Comparison children were read to no more than twice a week and focused nearly entirely on the basal and workbook. Free reading was allowed only when children had finished their basal seatwork.

Experimental children reported more reading of books and magazines after school and were able to name more favorite book titles and authors, suggesting that they did, in fact, do more reading. They also easily outperformed comparison children on a variety of tests, including story retelling, story rewriting, reading comprehension, and oral and written story creation. In addition, experimental students used a wider variety of words and more complicated sentences in their written story retellings. There was, however, no significant difference between the groups for total reading and language on a standardized test, the CTBS.

Gambrell (1996) reported on a study involving more than seven thousand first-grade children in forty-nine schools (see also Gambrell et al. 1995). About fifty to sixty new books were introduced per classroom, and children read or heard twenty-one books over a ten-week period. "Reading related" incentives, such as stickers and books, were used to encourage children to reach the twenty-one-book goal. Gambrell reported "statistically significant increases in reading motivation and behaviors" (18) compared to comparison children. A follow-up study with children from schools with low scores on tests of literacy was also successful: experimental children "were more motivated to read, spent more time reading independently, engaged more frequently in discussions about books and stories with family and friends, took more books home to read, and spent more time reading with family members" (28), as compared to comparison children. A third study confirmed that the effects of the ten-week program were present six months after the program ended. It can be argued that the incentives were the crucial aspect of the success of this program, but in view of other evidence that does not support incentives (McQuillan 1997), reading itself appears to be the likely candidate.

The Cincinnati Studies

A series of studies from the University of Cincinnati revealed clear differences in several aspects of literacy development as a result of participating in skills-based and literature-based classes. In all of these studies, a thorough description is provided of the methodology used in class. While skills-based classes included some literature (stories, free reading) and literature-based classes included some skills, the emphasis in the literature-based classes was clear: the comprehension and appreciation of interesting texts.

In Freppon (1995), second graders who had had "whole language" during kindergarten and grade one went on to either literature-based second-grade classes or skills-based second-grade classes. Freppon reported that both groups showed an increase "in use of written language characteristics and fluency during the second part of the second grade" (521), and there was no significant difference between the groups on a test of oral reading and retelling of a story. The literature students, were, however, more engaged in written language; they wrote more in school (Table 3–3) and read more at home. Interviews with parents confirmed these results. Parents of the children in the literature group

Table 3–3
Writing Produced at the End of the Second Grade
(Journal Writing, One Month)

	SKILLS-BASED CLASS	LITERATURE-BASED CLASS
Total number of written artifacts	17	39
Words per piece	38	59
Evidence of written language characteristics in writing	47%	90%

Source: Freppon (1995)

"stressed their children's keen interest in literacy" (523), while several of the parents in the skills-based group remarked that their children showed less interest in writing.

In Purcell-Gates, McIntyre, and Freppon (1995), skills-based and literature-based first graders from low-socioeconomic homes were asked to pretend to tell a story to a pretend five-year-old, and stories were analyzed for the presence of literary language (e.g., literary words and complex syntax). Table 3–4 presents one of their analyses, the number of literary devices used divided by the total number of intonation units.

While both groups gained, children in the whole language class made better gains in the use of literary language than children in the skills group. In addition, both groups closed in on the scores produced by children who had been read to a great deal outside of school. Note that the skills group showed clear gains as well. This is most likely due to the fact that they had been read to, but not as much as the literature students. Purcell-Gates,

Table 3–4
Use of Literary Language in Story Retellings

		OCCURRENCES	
	N	Beginning kindergarten	End of grade one
Well-read-to[a]	20	53	
Skills-based	33	28	56
Literature-based	24	21	60
[a]outside of school			

Source: Purcell-Gates, McIntyre, and Freppon (1995)

McIntyre, and Freppon suggest that the whole language students' greater development of the language used in books will make their reading much easier and will eventually result in greater literacy development.

The Foorman et al. Study

Foorman et al. (1997), in a study of Chapter 1 first and second graders, compared three approaches:

1. Direct Instruction (DI): DI provided "teacher-directed systematic instruction in a balanced program of reading instruction which includes phonemic awareness, phonics, and literature (68)."

2. Embedded Phonics (EP): In EP, "the emphasis was on phonemic awareness and spelling patterns (67)."

3. Whole Language (WL): In WL, "students are given a wide variety of opportunities to read, write, learn, and construct meaning within a meaningful context (67)."

The study reported that the DI group did better on the Woodcock-Johnson Basic Reading Test (letter-word identification and word attack) and on the Woodcock-Johnson Broad Reading Test (letter-word identification and passage comprehension). Only percentile ranks were provided, and they are presented here in Table 3–5. No differences were reported, however, on the Formal Reading Inventory, "a test of reading comprehension using narrative and expository text," and scores for all three groups were very low on this measure, ranging from the 6th to 22nd percentile.

This study is the only apparent counterexample to the generalization that students who do more real reading will outperform those who do less. This interpretation assumes, however, that the whole language students did, in fact, more real reading. The abysmal scores in reading comprehension (Formal Reading Inventory) suggest that none of the groups did much reading. In addition, full details of the study are lacking (but will appear in forthcoming studies by Foorman and her colleagues).

It could be argued that this study should be classified in the Other Definitions of Whole Language section, on page 38, as a

Table 3–5
Performance at the End of One Year (in Percentiles)

	DI	EP	WL
Basic reading	44	32	27
Broad reading	46	35	31
Formal Reading Inventory			
no extra tutorial	17	22	6
extra tutorial	10	11	10

Source: Foorman et al. (1997)

study in which a group is labeled as "whole language" but lacking evidence that the group did more real reading. The whole language group in this study engaged in "writing, spelling, and phonics instruction in context" in addition to "interactions in print-rich environments"; the embedded phonics curriculum included book reading, and the direct instruction curriculum (Open Court) is described as a balanced program that includes literature in addition to phonics and phonemic awareness. The literature component included shared reading of big books and the use of text anthologies with uncontrolled vocabulary.

Knapp with Adelman et al. (1995) studied sixty-six classrooms "serving large numbers of children from low-income families" (xi). Classes were analyzed according to their orientation to meaning. Specifically, in meaning-oriented classes, there was:

1. More time devoted to reading. In high-meaning emphasis classes, children read an average of forty-eight minutes per day; in medium-meaning emphasis, eighteen minutes per day; and in low-meaning emphasis, five minutes per day. No mention was made as to whether the reading was self-selected or assigned.

2. Integrated reading and writing.

3. Focus on meaning.

4. Discussion of what was read.

For the first year of the project, sixteen classes were classified as high-meaning emphasis, twenty-nine as medium, and twenty-two as low.

Table 3–6 presents differences in achievement on the CTBS reading comprehension test in terms of gains, with pretest CTBS scores used as covariates (Knapp et al. 1995). Only the two extreme groups are presented: the classes highest in meaning emphasis and those lowest. While children in the meaning em-

Table 3–6

Differences in NCEs on the CTBS Reading Comprehension Test

DURATION	GRADES	N	GAINS IN NCES
first year of project:			
One academic year, fall to spring	1, 3, 5	1068	+5.6
Twelve months, fall to fall	1, 3, 5	477	−.5
second year of project:			
One academic year, fall to spring	2, 4, 6	1123	+1.4
12 months, spring to spring	2, 4, 6	415	+3.3

+ = high-meaning emphasis superior
− = low-meaning emphasis superior
NCE = normal curve equivalent

Source: Knapp et al. (1995)

phasis classes did better, the results were not statistically significant, except for the 5.6 NCE gain achieved by the first, third, and fifth graders over one academic year for the first year of the project. In a comparison of moderate-emphasis classes to low-meaning emphasis classes, done over one academic year, the moderate-emphasis classes made significantly larger gains: 4.0 NCEs in one sample and 3.9 NCEs in a second (Knapp with Adelman et al., 228).

Knapp et al. also administered the Woodcock word-attack subtest to determine the impact of meaning emphasis instruction on discrete skills (Table 3–7). The low-meaning emphasis group appeared to be better in one sample, while the high-meaning emphasis group did better in another sample, but neither difference was statistically significant.

Table 3–7

Mastery of Skills: Performance on Word-Attack (Woodcock)

DURATION	GRADES	N	GAINS IN NCE'S
One academic year, fall to spring	1, 3, 5	135	–6.8
One academic year, fall to spring	2, 4, 6	137	+5.7

(pretest CTBS reading used as covariate)
+ = high-meaning emphasis superior
– = low-meaning emphasis superior

Source: Knapp et al. (1995)

Summary

This set of studies suggests that students who do more real reading have better attitudes toward reading (McKenna et al. 1995; Merver and Hiebert 1989; Gambrell 1996), read more (Freppon 1995; Gambrell 1996), do as well as traditional students on tests in which the focus is on form, do as well or better on more communicative tests (Merver and Hiebert 1989; Hagerty et al. 1989; Morrow, O'Connor, and Smith (1990); Klesius et al. 1991; Morrow 1992) and show better development of the kind of language used in books (Freppon 1995; Purcell-Gates, McIntyre, and Freppon 1995). Foorman et al. (1997) is the only study in which skills-emphasis children do better. Table 3–8 summarizes these results.

Other Definitions of Whole Language

When we define whole language as providing children with comprehensible and interesting texts, and helping them understand these texts, whole language does very well in method comparison studies. These results are consistent with findings showing the effectiveness of sustained silent reading and other methods that

Table 3–8
Summary

			MEASURES			
study	RC	skills	amount read	attitude	literate language	story (re)telling
McKenna et al.				WL		
Merver & Hiebert			WL			
Morrow et al.	WL	nd				
Eldredge	WL	WL		WL		
Klesius et al.	nd	nd				
Morrow	nd/WL	nd	WL			WL
Gambrell			WL	WL		
Freppon			WL	WL		nd
Purcell-Gates et al.					WL	
Foorman et al.	sk	sk				
Knapp with Adelman et al.	nd/WL	nd				

WL = whole language group superior
nd = no difference
sk = skills group superior
Note that in Morrow, WL students were superior in one reading comprehension test, but were equal in the CTBS reading test, which includes a reading comprehension test.

provide students with large quantities of comprehensible text, when treatments are done for a long enough duration.

On the other hand, when whole language is not defined as real reading, it does not do well when compared to skills-based methods. In the studies described in this section, "whole language" in some cases is clearly not based on the comprehension hypothesis, and in others we have no idea whether the "whole language" group did more real reading than the comparison group.

Holland and Hall (1989) reported no differences in reading achievement between a basal and "whole language" approach for first-grade children after one year. Many aspects of the whole language class, however, had little to do with helping children understand interesting text. The emphasis appeared to be on deliberate vocabulary development and a focus on words in isolation. The whole language method differed from the traditional largely in how the target words were selected (e.g., volunteered by students rather than in prepared lists), and the fact that skills were not taught in a prescribed sequence but "as needed." Nevertheless, the whole language group focused on isolated word meanings and direct teaching of skills.

Reutzel and Cooper (1990), in a study of first graders, present results favorable to whole language, but once again it is not clear whether whole language students read more than "basal" students. While the whole language students clearly read a great deal, so did the comparison students: They were read to daily and "toward the end of the year children were encouraged to read silently books of their own choosing" (254). In addition, reading outside of school was encouraged in both programs.

Foorman et al. (1991) compared first graders in "language experience" classes with first graders in classes with more emphasis on letter-sound correspondences. While the study describes the language experience classes as emphasizing "whole words in meaningful contexts" (458), there is no evidence that they did more reading. Both groups used a basal series. Whole-word activities were contrived and did not entail real reading:

> Every day a different story was selected from the Harcourt Brace Jovanovitch series. The story provided a theme around which instruction was based. For example, if the theme was "bears" and the goal was to teach about verbs, then the teacher and the children might brainstorm about the following "story starter": The bear was _____ the honey. Pointing at a big picture of a bear on the bulletin board, the teacher might ask, "What might a bear do with honey?" New vocabulary words from the Harcourt Brace Jovanovitch stories were written on tagboard and stored in a word bank. During reading group time, the day's story was rebuilt with sentence strips, which were written on tagboard. (458)

While the language experience class appeared to have some exposure to comprehensible text, clearly a great deal of time was devoted to activities other than reading. There was no difference between the groups in gains in phonemic awareness, and the letter-sound emphasis group was significantly better in spelling and word reading. No test of reading comprehension was used.

Foorman et al. (1998) has similar problems. First and second graders receiving Title 1 services were in one of three groups: a "direct code" group that had "direct instruction in letter-sound correspondences practiced in decodable texts" (39); an "embedded code" group that had "less direct instruction in systematic spelling patterns [onset rimes] embedded in connected text" (39); and an "indirect, incidental instruction" group for which "the alphabetic code [was] embedded in connected text" (39). The direct code group did best on a measure of decoding at the end of the year as well as on a sentence-level cloze test (labeled "passage comprehension"). There was no

difference on a spelling test, nor on a test of reading comprehension, but the latter test suffered from a floor effect: It was
too difficult for all the groups. The "indirect" group had significantly more positive attitudes toward reading than the direct
code group.

All three groups "existed within a literature-rich environment in the classroom" (39). The third group, "indirect, incidental
instruction" was considered to follow a "whole language" philoso-
phy, but there was direct instruction in the alphabetic code. Instead of following a prescribed syllabus, however, "the teacher
used shared- and guided-reading activities to draw children's attention to specific words or word forms, letters, sounds, patterns,
meanings, making predictions, listening to rhymes, and exploring
the use of strategies, grammar, language use, spellings, or key
ideas in the text" (40). There is no evidence that this group did
any more real reading for meaning than the others.

Hiebert et al. (1992) compared Chapter 1 first graders who
participated in two programs:

1. The "restructured" program had three components: "(a)
    reading of predictable books, (b) writing rhyming words and
    journal writing, and (c) strategic guidance about patterns of
    words" (555), the latter focusing on the use of analogy.

2. The regular Chapter 1 program was described as "whole lan-
    guage," with an emphasis on shared reading and "lessons that
    aid children in strategies like using context clues and making
    predictions" (553). The regular program also included direct
    instruction in word recognition, word analysis, and "struc-
    tural analysis" (553).

The restructured group easily outperformed the regular
group on a variety of measures, including standardized tests. It
was not at all clear, however, that the "whole language" group did
more reading. While Hiebert et al. note that in the regular group

"funds were spent on sets of books" rather than for a textbook series (553), children in the restructured group, in addition to reading predictable books in class, "were encouraged to take books home nightly, with parents signing a card to verify children's reading. To foster the development of home libraries for children, a trade book publisher contributed a box of books, from which children chose one for their home libraries whenever they completed a card of 10 nightly readings" (556).

Stahl, McKenna, and Pagnucco (1994) report effect sizes for four studies in which whole language and traditional instruction were compared on standardized measures of reading comprehension, and report a small advantage for whole language ($d = .08$). Using a larger sample of studies, all in which reading was measured in some way, they reported that whole language students were better in four studies, traditional methodology was better in one study, and no difference was found in twelve studies. While all studies analyzed are listed in their bibliography, they do not tell us which studies were used in their analysis. In addition, many of the studies are unpublished. We thus have no idea what "whole language" meant in this analysis.

Biemiller and Siegel is summarized in Biemiller (1994). It is a comparison of "Bridge Reading" and whole language. Very little information is provided in this report, but Biemiller concludes that the results are consistent with findings showing basal programs are more effective than whole language. In Bridge Reading, an "additional scaffold context for acquiring sight words" is provided (205). In beginning primers, pictures illustrating the meanings of words are provided, along with supplementary activities. Gradually, the pictures are removed and the child can read subsequent texts without them. As Biemiller notes, the whole language comparison groups were not well described. While no data is provided in Biemiller, if the Bridge Readers actually did better, it is not a surprise. Bridge Reading appears to be a way of making beginning texts highly comprehensible. It may be the case that children in the Bridge Reading group experienced more comprehensible text than the children in "whole language."

McGuinness, McGuinness, and Donohue (1995) compared children ages six to eight in two experimental classes who experienced direct instruction in phonological awareness for eight months emphasizing conscious knowledge of place and manner of articulation of sounds for twenty to thirty minutes per day (the Lindamood Auditory Discrimination in Depth program) with a comparison group utilizing a "modified whole language" approach. One of the experimental classes was from a Montessori school and the other also used a "modified whole language" approach. Both experimental classes made superior gains on tests involving word identification and reading nonsense words. No test of reading comprehension was used. "Whole language" had, apparently, little to do with real reading. According to McGuinness, McGuinness, and Donohue, the teacher in the comparison group

> spent 45 minutes per day in story time, which was the main language activity in the classroom. Children wrote a story which could be continued on the following day. The teacher walked around the room during this activity and answered any questions and spelled a word if she was asked. . . . When the stories were completed, students could illustrate their stories and create a book binding. Students who finished work could read a book or select from the worksheets. (846)

Eldredge and Baird (1996), in a paper entitled "Phonemic Awareness Training Works Better than Whole Language Instruction for Teaching First Graders How to Write," used a definition of whole language that is hard to interpret in terms of any hypothesis. The "whole language" group used a "holistic approach" to learning to write, which combined language experience, copying language experience stories, "studying" the words and sentences in the stories, creating word banks, and using the words in writing activities and classroom games. The same children also "were taught to read" using a basal reader (198). Language experience provided some comprehensible text, but the other activities are clearly not related to the comprehension hypothesis.

Traw (1996) found no differences in standardized test scores in two districts after "whole language" was introduced. Whole language was defined as teaching skills in context, as assuming the similarity between oral and written language, as assuming that all modes are "interrelated and mutually reinforcing" (324), and as a recognition that "learning is developmental but idiosyncratic" (324). It is quite possible that whole language students in these districts did more real reading after whole language was introduced; Traw reports that one district "invested heavily in trade books" and the other allowed teachers to use funds for trade books rather than workbooks, and that 90 percent of the teachers did this. There is no discussion, however, of whether whole language students read more.

Sacks and Mergendoller (1997) compared kindergarten classes categorized as "whole language" and "phonics." It is not clear that the whole language children had more interaction with comprehensible text:

PERCENTAGE OF TIME:	WHOLE LANGUAGE	PHONICS
Time looking through books silently	6.3	15.8
Time attending to environmental or nonbook print	40.4	29.3
Total time interacting with comprehensible text	46.7	45.1

The phonics group clearly spent more time with worksheets, a total of 19.4 percent, compared to 6.9 percent, and spent less time using invented spelling (1.1 percent compared to 10.4 percent).

The test used was not a test of reading comprehension, but was the Test of Early Reading (TERA), which did include "constructing meaning from print" (725). Sacks and Mergendoller reported no difference for higher-scoring students, while the whole language low-scoring children did slightly better than the low-scoring phonics children.

LOW	WHOLE LANGUAGE	PHONICS
Pretest	11.7 (1.92)	10.3 (2.53)
Posttest	21.7 (3.22)	18.5 (1.95)
HIGH	WHOLE LANGUAGE	PHONICS
Pretest	20.4 (1.24)	20.0 (2.73)
Posttest	26.8 (1.42)	27.6 (2.09)

While one could argue that the whole language group had more exposure to comprehensible texts, because silent reading at this age may not be comprehensible, this is speculation. The most likely interpretation is that differences in exposure to comprehensible text were small, which explains why differences in test scores were small. What is clear is that the extra worksheet time did not help the phonics children, and the time using invented spelling did not hurt the whole language children. The study thus provides evidence against "skill building," and thus provides indirect support for the comprehension hypothesis.

Summary and Conclusion

Method comparison studies that involve groups that clearly differ in the amount of real reading done present results consistent with studies of older children and adults: More reading typically results in better literacy development. This is exactly what the comprehension hypothesis predicts, and it is strong support for "whole language" when whole language is understood to have as a major goal providing children with interesting texts and helping them understand these texts.[2]

Notes

1. The "skills" group did about as much or more reading than the "non-skills" group in Harris and Serwer (1966) and Evans and Carr (1985). See McQuillan (1998) for detailed discussion of these and other studies in which the non-skills groups actually had little exposure to comprehensible text.

2. Honig (1996) cites Goldenberg (1994) as showing that "direct instruction in phonics [in Spanish] for Spanish-speaking kindergarten children produced significantly higher reading in first grade and beyond and was the most productive of all the methods he tried" (38). A close look at Goldenberg's research shows this is not the case. Goldenberg's study is described in detail in Goldenberg, Reese, and Gallimore (1992) and included only two groups of five children. Experimental (Libro) children heard stories in class and took the books home. A total of twelve books was used, each consisting of five to ten pages of text, with one book introduced every three weeks. Experimental children also learned the alphabet and went through the regular district reading readiness program. Control children took home worksheets that focused on skills. Contrary to Honig's description, experimental children outperformed control children on posttests (including letter identification and word reading) given at the end of the year.

Honig's conclusion may have been based on the finding that for the comparison group, there was a positive and significant correlation between the amount of use of the materials brought home and performance on the posttests. This group, however, was not better. Parents of experimental group children did not use the books as intended: Rather than using them as storybooks, they corrected the children as they read aloud and "virtually no attention [was] paid to relationships between print and meaning" (515). This may have been the reason why no relationship was found between the time devoted to the use of the books at home and posttest performance. As Goldenberg, Reese, and Gallimore note, one interpretation of the findings is that "classroom use, and not home use, was the crucial feature that explained the superior early reading achievement of the Libro children" (528).

Several studies provide what seems to be mixed and inconclusive results on the impact of in-school reading on reading achievement. These studies have several features in common: They all deal with elementary school children; all rely on observations of classrooms; and all attempt to relate the amount of silent reading done with reading achievement, while controlling for students' initial reading achievement at the beginning of the observation period. (This control is necessary, since there is a tendency for teachers to allow more-able students to do more free reading, as shown by Allington 1980).

One study found a negative relationship between time spent reading and reading achievement (Stallings 1980, secondary school students), one found no relationship (Haynes and Jenkins 1986, "mildly handicapped" fourth, fifth, and sixth graders), and two studies reported a positive relationship (Leinhardt, Zigmond, and Cooley 1981, "learning disabled" children, ages six to twelve; Taylor, Frye, and Maruyama 1990, grades five and six), but data from one of these studies (Leinhardt, Zigmond, and Cooley) was reanalyzed and the positive relationship disappeared (Wilkinson, Wardrop, and Anderson 1988). Also, one study presenting simple correlations showed small correlations between silent reading time and achievement (Evans and Carr 1985, $r = .17$, overall individualized silent reading), while another showed a positive relationship (Harris and Serwer 1966, $r = .55$).

There are several possible causes for this failure of silent reading to show a consistent effect. First, silent reading in these studies was not necessarily meaningful reading. It included reading single words or even single letters. Even if silent reading did consist of reading meaningful text, these texts could very well have been assigned "reading comprehension" exercises, comprehensible but not very interesting. Another possible problem is that relatively little time was devoted to silent reading in these studies: The range for daily reading was from about six minutes per period in Haynes and Jenkins to about fifteen minutes in other studies, and the overall duration was typically about four months. It may take more reading than this to show an effect (Krashen 1993).

References

Allington, R. 1980. "Poor Readers Don't Get to Read Much in Reading Groups." *Language Arts* 57: 872–876.

Biemiller, A. 1994. "Some Observations of Beginning Reading Instruction." *Educational Psychologist* 29 (4): 203–209.

Eldredge, L. 1991. "An Experiment with a Modified Whole Language Approach in First-Grade Classrooms." *Reading Research and Instruction,* 30 (3): 21–38.

Eldredge, L., and J. Baird. 1996. "Phonemic Awareness Training Works Better than Whole Language Instruction for Teaching First Graders How to Write." *Reading Research and Instruction* 35: 193–208.

Elley, W. 1991. "Acquiring Literacy in a Second Language: The Effect of Book-Based Programs." *Language Learning* 41 (3): 375–411.

Evans, M., and T. Carr. 1985. "Cognitive Abilities, Conditions of Learning, and the Early Development of Reading Skill." *Reading Research Quarterly* 20: 327–350.

Foorman, B., D. Francis, T. Beeler, D. Winikates, and J. Fletcher. 1997. "Early Intervention for Children with Reading Problems: Study Designs and Preliminary Findings." *Learning Disabilities* 8:63–71.

Foorman, B., D. Francis, J. Fletcher, C. Schatschneider, and P. Mehta. 1998. "The Role of Instruction in Learning to Read: Preventing

Reading Failure in At-Risk Children." *Journal of Educational Psychology* 90 (1): 37–55.

Foorman, B., D. Francis, D. Novy, and D. Liberman. 1991. "How Letter-Sound Instruction Mediates Progress in First-Grade Reading and Spelling." *Journal of Educational Psychology* 83: 456–469.

Foorman, B., L. Jenkins, and D. Francis. 1993. "Links Among Segmenting, Spelling, and Reading Words in First and Second Graders." *Reading and Writing* 5: 1–15.

Freppon, P. 1995. "Low-Income Children's Literacy Interpretations in a Skills-Based and Whole-Language Classroom." *Journal of Reading Behavior* 27: 505–533.

Gambrell, L. 1996. "Creating Classroom Cultures that Foster Reading Motivation." *The Reading Teacher* 50: 14–25.

Gambrell, L., J. Almasi, Q. Xie, and V. Heland. 1995. "Helping First Graders Get a Running Start in Reading." In *Family Literacy,* ed. L. Morrow, 143–154. Newark, DE: International Reading Association.

Goldenberg, C. 1994. "Promoting Early Literacy Development Among Spanish-Speaking Children: Lessons from Two Studies." In *Getting Reading Right from the Start: Effective Early Literacy Intervention,* ed. E. H. Hiebert and B. M. Taylor, 171–199. Boston: Allyn & Bacon.

Goldenberg, C., L. Reese, and R. Gallimore. 1992. "Effects of Literacy Materials from School on Latin Children's Home Experiences and Early Reading Achievement." *American Journal of Education* 100: 497–536.

Goodman, K. 1982. *Language and Literacy: The Selected Writings of Kenneth S. Goodman.* Boston: Routledge & Kegan Paul.

Hagerty, P., E. Hiebert, and M. Owens. 1989. "Students' Comprehension, Writing, and Perceptions in Two Approaches to Literacy Instruction." In *Cognitive and Social Perspectives for Literacy Research and Instruction: Thirty-Eighth Yearbook of the National Reading Conference,* ed. B. McCormick and J. Zutell, 453–459. Chicago: National Reading Conference.

Harris, A., and B. Serwer. 1966. "The CRAFT Project: Instructional Time in Reading Research." *Reading Research Quarterly* 2 (1): 27–57.

Haynes, M., and J. Jenkins. 1986. "Reading Instruction in Special Education Resource Rooms." *American Educational Research Journal* 23: 161–190.

Hiebert, E., J. Colt, S. Catto, and E. Gury. 1992. "Reading and Writing of First-Grade Students in a Restructured Chapter 1 Program." *American Educational Research Journal* 29: 545–572.

Holland, K., and L. Hall. 1989. "Reading Achievement in First Grade Classrooms: A Comparison of Basal and Whole Language Approaches." *Reading Improvement* 26: 323–329.

Honig, B. 1996. *Teaching Our Children to Read.* Thousand Oaks, CA: Kern Press.

Klesius, J., P. Griffith, and P. Zielonka. 1991. "A Whole Language and Traditional Instruction Comparison: Overall Effectiveness and Development of the Alphabetic Principle." *Reading Research and Instruction* 30: 47–61.

Knapp, M., with N. E. Adelman et al. 1995. *Teaching for Meaning in High-Poverty Classrooms.* New York: Teachers College Press.

Knapp, M., C. Marder, A. Zucker, N. Adelman, and M. Needels. 1995. "The Outcomes of Teaching for Meaning in High-Poverty Classrooms." In *Teaching for Meaning in High-Poverty Classrooms,* ed. M. Knapp with N. E. Adelman et al., 124–159. New York: Teachers College Press.

Krashen, S. 1985. *The Input Hypothesis.* Beverly Hills: Laredo Publishing Company.

———. 1993. *The Power of Reading.* Englewood, CO: Libraries Unlimited.

Leinhardt, G., N. Zigmond, and W. Cooley. 1981. "Reading Instruction and Its Effects." *American Educational Research Journal* 18: 343–361.

Mason, B., and S. Krashen. 1997. "Extensive Reading in English as a Foreign Language." *System* 25: 91–102.

McGuinness, D., C. McGuinness, and J. Donohue. 1995. "Phonological Training and the Alphabet Principle: Evidence for Reciprocal Causality." *Reading Research Quarterly* 30: 830–852.

McKenna, M., B. Stratton, M. Grindler, and S. Jenkins. 1995. "Differential

Effects of Whole Language and Traditional Instruction on Reading Attitudes." *Journal of Reading Behavior* 27: 19–44.

McQuillan, J. 1997. "The Effects of Incentives on Reading." *Reading Research and Instruction* 36 (2): 111–125.

———. 1998. *The Literacy Crisis: False Claims and Real Solutions.* Portsmouth, NH: Heinemann.

Merver, K. and E. Hiebert. 1989. "Literature-Selection Strategies and Amount of Reading in Two Literacy Approaches." In *Cognitive and Social Perspectives for Literacy Research and Instruction: Thirty-Eighth Yearbook of the National Reading Conference,* ed. S. McCormick and J. Zutell, 529–535. Chicago: National Reading Conference.

Morrow, L. 1992. "The Impact of a Literature-Based Program on Literacy Achievement, Use of Literature, and Attitudes of Children from Minority Backgrounds." *Reading Research Quarterly* 27: 250–275.

———. 1996. "Motivating Reading and Writing in Diverse Classrooms." In *NCTE Research Report No. 28.* Urbana, IL: National Council of Teachers of English.

Morrow, L., E. O'Connor, and J. Smith. 1990. "Effects of a Story Reading Program on the Literacy Development of At-Risk Kindergarten Children." *Journal of Reading Behavior* 22: 255–275.

Purcell-Gates, V., E. McIntyre, and P. Freppon. 1995. "Learning Written Storybook Language in School: A Comparison of Low-SES Children in Skills-Based and Whole Language Classrooms." *American Educational Research Journal* 32: 659–685.

Reutzel, D., and R. Cooper. 1990. "Whole Language: Comparative Effects on First-Grade Reading Achievement." *Journal of Educational Research* 83: 252–257.

Sacks, C., and J. Mergendoller. 1997. "The Relationship Between Teachers' Theoretical Orientation Toward Reading and Student Outcomes in Kindergarten Children with Different Initial Reading Abilities." *American Educational Research Journal* 34 (4): 721–739.

Smith, F. 1994. *Understanding Reading,* 5th ed. Hillsdale, NJ: Erlbaum.

Stahl, S. 1994. "Separating the Rhetoric from the Effects: Whole Language in Kindergarten and First Grade." In *Reading, Language, and Literacy,* ed. F. Leer and J. Osborne, 101–114. Hillsdale, NJ: Erlbaum.

Stahl, S., M. McKenna, and J. Pagnucco. 1994. "The Effects of Whole-Language Instruction: An Update and Reappraisal." *Educational Psychologist* 29 (4): 175–185.

Stallings, J. 1980. "Allocated Academic Learning Time Revisited, or Beyond Time on Task." *Educational Researcher* 9: 11–16.

Taylor, B., B. Frye, and G. Maruyama. 1990. "Time Spent Reading and Reading Growth." *American Educational Research Journal* 27: 351–362.

Traw, R. 1996. "Large-Scale Assessment of Skills in a Whole Language Curriculum: Two Districts' Experiences." *The Journal of Educational Research* 89: 323–339.

Wilkinson, I., J. Wardrop, and R. Anderson. 1988. "Silent Reading Reconsidered: Reinterpreting Reading Instruction and Its Effects." *American Educational Research Journal* 25: 127–144.

4

Eliminating Print Deprivation

The provision of a rich supply of high-interest story books is a much more feasible policy for improving English learning than any pious pronouncements about the urgent need to raise teacher quality.

—FRANCIS MANGUBHAI AND WARWICK ELLEY,
"THE ROLE OF READING IN PROMOTING ESL"

The previous chapters of this book have been devoted to analyzing the arguments against whole language. I now turn to what I think is the major part of the cure of any "literacy crisis": supplying good reading and a comfortable place to read.

Free Voluntary Reading

Much of our competence in reading and in literacy in general comes from one source: free voluntary reading. Free reading profoundly improves our reading ability, our writing ability, our spelling, our grammar, and our vocabulary. This conclusion comes from the following kinds of evidence:

Reading More Improves Literacy Development

Those who say they read more typically have superior literacy development. Correlations between the amount of self-reported reading people do and scores of measures of literacy achievement are nearly always positive. I report here on some recent additions to this research.

In Stokes, Krashen, and Kartchner (in press), students of Spanish as a foreign language in the United States were tested on their knowledge of the subjunctive on a test that attempted to probe naturally acquired competence (in the results that follow, only subjects who were not aware that the subjunctive was the focus of the test were included). Formal study was not a predictor of subjunctive competence, nor was length of residence in a Spanish-speaking country. The study also asked subjects about the quality of instruction they had had specifically in the subjunctive. This variable also failed to predict performance on the subjunctive test. The amount of free reading, in Spanish, however, was a clear predictor (Table 4–1).

Table 4–1
Predictors of Performance on the Subjunctive in Spanish

PREDICTOR	BETA	T	P
Formal study	.0518	.36	.718
Length of residence	.0505	.35	.726
Amount of reading	.3222	2.19	.034
Subject study	.0454	.31	.757

$r^2 = .12, p = .128$

Source: Stokes, Krashen, and Kartchner (in press)

Lee, Krashen, and Gribbons (1996) reported that for international students in the United States, the amount of free reading reported (number of years subjects read newspapers, news magazines, popular magazines, fiction, and nonfiction) was a significant predictor of the ability to translate and judge the grammaticality of complex grammatical constructions in English (restrictive relative clauses). The amount of formal study and length of residence in the United States were not significant predictors. Results for the grammaticality judgment task are presented in Table 4–2 (translation results were similar).

Constantino et al. (1997) reported that the amount of free reading international students living in the United States said they did before taking the TOEFL was an excellent predictor of their score on this examination (Table 4–3). In this study, formal study and length of residence were also significant (and independent) predictors.

The Author Recognition Test

Stanovich and his colleagues have introduced a simple test format for measuring the amount of reading people do. In the Author

Table 4–2

Grammaticality Judgment Test (Simultaneous Regression)

PREDICTOR	BETA	T	P
Amount of reading	.516	3.98	.0002
Formal study	.072	.57	.568
Length of residence	.052	.40	.690

$r^2 = .29, p < .05$

Source: Lee, Gribbons, and Krashen (1996)

Table 4–3
Predictors of Performance on the TOEFL Test
(Simultaneous Regression)

PREDICTOR	BETA	T	P
Free reading/books	.41	3.422	.002
English study/home	.48	3.726	.001
Length of residence in the United States	.42	3.243	.003
$r^2 = .45$			

Source: Constantino et al. (1997)

Recognition Test (ART), Magazine Recognition Test (MRT), and Title Recognition Test (TRT) subjects simply indicate whether they recognize authors, magazines, or book titles. Performance on these tests is consistently related to levels of literacy for English as a first language. Performance on the Author Recognition Test, for example, correlates with measures of vocabulary (Stanovich, West, and Harrison 1995; West, Stanovich, and Mitchell 1993; Lee, Krashen, and Tse 1997), reading comprehension (Stanovich and West 1989), and spelling (Cunningham and Stanovich 1990). Scores on the ART also correlate with how much reading people are observed doing (West, Stanovich, and Mitchell 1993), as well as with the amount of reading people say they do (Allen, Cipielewski, and Stanovich 1992).

These tests work in other languages as well: Lee and Krashen (1996) found a modest but positive correlation between performance on the ART in Chinese and scores on the composition section of the Senior High School Entrance Examination for secondary students in Taiwan, and Rodrigo, McQuillan, and Krashen (1996) reported a positive correlation between performance on a Spanish language ART and vocabulary knowledge for adult native speakers of Spanish. Finally, there is recent evidence that the ART and MRT given in English are predictors of English vocabulary for high school students studying English as a foreign language in Korea (Kim and Krashen, in press).

Sweet Valley High

In addition to correlational studies, strong evidence confirming the power of reading comes from case histories of readers. Cho and Krashen (1994) reported on the effect of reading novels from the Sweet Valley High series on adult second language acquisition. Three subjects in this study had studied English formally for a substantial amount of time in Korea and had lived in the United States for several years, but they reported severe difficulty in using English. A fourth subject was a native speaker of Spanish who had higher proficiency in English.

We suggested to our subjects that they begin their English reading program with novels from the Sweet Valley High series. Sweet Valley High novels, part of a genre known as "adolescent fiction" (or sometimes "teen romance"), are written for junior high and high school girls and are written at the sixth-grade level. The original Sweet Valley series proved to be too difficult, so we suggested Sweet Valley Twins, at the fourth-grade level, and eventually Sweet Valley Kids, at the second-grade level. Our subjects, women in their thirties, became fanatic Sweet Valley Kids readers. They reported enjoying the reading enormously, made impressive gains on tests of vocabulary, and reported great improvement in their English.

In Cho and Krashen (1995a), we reported on the progress of one of the original four subjects, Mi-ae, who continued reading Sweet Valley High novels. Before starting to read the Sweet Valley series, she had lived in the United States for five years and had studied English as a foreign language for six years. Nevertheless, she told us that she had difficulty understanding native speakers and television, was afraid of talking on the telephone, and was reluctant to engage English speakers in conversation. Over a period of seven and a half months, Mi-ae read thirty-nine Sweet Valley Kids novels and four novels from the Sweet Valley Twins series, the first real pleasure reading she had ever done in English. She also, during this time, started reading magazines such as *Vogue, People,* and the *National Enquirer.*

Her progress was obvious. She supplied her own test of listening comprehension: "I had two movie video tapes. I did not understand them at all five years ago, and just looked at the pictures. I did not understand them two years ago either. Last Tuesday, I watched them again to see if I could understand them. I understood them from the start. I could not catch everything, but I understood the entire story. I was so happy that I could understand words that I knew from the reading, such as *envy, avoid,* and *wet*" (translated from Korean by Kyung-Sook Cho).

We also have informal evidence that Mi-ae's speaking ability in English improved. My coauthor, Kyung-Sook Cho, spoke to an English speaker who had been doing business with Mi-ae for the previous ten months. He noticed a change: "When my wife and I met her last year, she fumbled for words. Now she speaks easily, without hesitation ... my wife and I both noticed that Mi-ae is now very confident in speaking English." Interestingly, he also inquired whether Mi-ae had been studying English formally.

Another case history (Cho and Krashen 1995b) is Karen. Like Mi-ae, Karen had studied English in Korea. In the United States, she studied ESL, but dropped the class because of the emphasis on grammar. Like Mi-ae, she was an avid pleasure reader in Korean, but had never attempted pleasure reading in English, associating reading with hard work and the difficult texts used in EFL and ESL classes. In a one-year period, she read twenty-five Sweet Valley Kids novels, twenty-one Sweet Valley Twins novels, and twenty novels from the Sweet Valley High series. This is roughly one million words, which is about the number of words middle-class children read in one year in English as a first language, combining reading done in school and outside of school (Anderson, Wilson, and Fielding 1988). During this time, Karen also read about forty copies of the *National Enquirer,* four Harlequin romances, and eight novels by Danielle Steele and Sidney Sheldon.

Like Mi-ae, Karen supplied her own reading comprehension test. She told us that when she came to the United States, she brought ten novels with her to improve her English. But, she said, "I could not read them at all . . . I was exhausted before finishing one page . . . it took me more time to look up the words in a bilingual dictionary than reading itself, and I still couldn't understand the text. Since then I have not touched them . . ." (translated from Korean). At the end of the year, she tried reading the novels she brought five years ago. She could now read them—they now looked "simple and understandable without any strain."

Additional evidence of her progress is the fact that she was able to read much more difficult books as she read more, moving from Sweet Valley Kids, written at the second-grade level, to popular novels written at the seventh-grade level. Karen read one popular novel in only four days at the end of the year.

Other Examples

Segal (1997) describes the case of L., a seventeen-year-old eleventh-grade student in Israel. L. speaks English at home with her parents, who are from South Africa, but had serious problems in English writing, especially in spelling, vocabulary, and writing style. Segal, L.'s teacher in grade ten, tried a variety of approaches:

> Error correction proved a total failure. L. tried correcting her own mistakes, tried process writing, and tried just copying

words correctly in her notebook. Nothing worked. L.'s compositions were poorly expressed and her vocabulary was weak. We conferenced together over format and discussed ideas before writing. We made little progress. I gave L. a list of five useful words to spell each week for six weeks and tested her in an unthreatening way during recess. L. performed well in the tests in the beginning, but by the end of six weeks she reverted to misspelling the words she had previously spelled correctly.

In addition, L.'s mother got her a private tutor, but there was little improvement.

Segal also taught L. in grade eleven. At the beginning of the year, she assigned an essay: "When I came to L.'s composition I stopped still. Before me was an almost perfect essay. There were no spelling mistakes. The paragraphs were clearly marked. Her ideas were well put and she made good sense. Her vocabulary had improved. I was amazed but at the same time uneasy . . ."

Segal discovered the reason for L.'s improvement: She had become a reader over the summer. L. told her, "I never read much before but this summer I went to the library and I started reading and I just couldn't stop." L.'s performance in grade eleven in English was consistently excellent and her reading habit has continued.

Cohen (1997) attended an English-language medium school in her native Turkey, beginning at age twelve. The first two years were devoted to intensive English study, and Cohen reports that after only two months, she started to read in English:

> as many books in English as I could get hold of. I had a rich, ready made library of English books at home. . . . I became a member of the local British Council's library and occasionally purchased English books in bookstores. . . . By the first year of middle school I had become an avid reader of English.

Her reading, however, led to an "unpleasant incident" in middle school:

> I had a new English teacher who assigned us two compositions for homework. She returned them to me ungraded, furious. She wanted to know who had helped me write them. They were my personal work. I had not even used the dictionary. She would not believe me. She pointed at a few underlined sentences and some vocabulary and asked me how I knew them; they were well beyond the level of the class. I had not even participated much in class. I was devastated. There and then and many years later I could not explain how I knew them. I just did.

Free Reading Programs Surpass Skill-Oriented Programs

In-school free reading programs such as sustained silent reading (SSR), in which children select their own reading material and are not tested on what they have read, have been shown to be consistently superior to skill-oriented programs in literacy development, as long as the programs run for a minimum of about one academic year (Krashen 1993).

Perhaps the best-known of in-school free reading programs is the Hooked on Books study (McNeil, in Fader 1976). The subjects were reform school boys, juvenile delinquents. The boys in the Hooked on Books program were each given a paperback book, which they could exchange for another paperback anytime. They were encouraged to read whatever they wanted to read, and there was no accountability. After two years the boys were tested and compared to reform schools boys who were not in the program. The readers improved in everything measured: reading comprehension, writing fluency, writing complexity, self-esteem, and attitude toward school. Control subjects stayed the same or got worse on these measures.

Reviews of SSR in the United States are available (Krashen 1993). I focus here on programs in other countries. The results demonstrate that free reading works all over the world.

In Elley and Mangubhai (1983), fourth- and fifth-grade students of English as a foreign language were divided into three groups for their thirty-minute daily English class. One group had traditional audio-lingual method instruction, a second did only free reading, while a third did "shared reading." Shared reading is "a method of sharing a good book with a class, several times, in such a way that the students are read to by the teacher, as in a bedtime story. They then talk about the book, they read it together, they act out the story, they draw parts of it and write their own caption, they rewrite the story with different characters or events" (Elley 1998). After two years, the free reading group and the shared reading group were far superior to the traditional group in tests of reading comprehension, writing, and grammar. Similar results were obtained by Elley (1991) in a large-scale study of second language acquirers ages six through nine in Singapore.

Elley's recent data (Elley 1998) comes from South Africa and Sri Lanka. In all cases, children who were encouraged to read for pleasure outperformed traditionally taught students on standardized tests of reading comprehension and other measures of literacy. Table 4–4 presents the data from South Africa. In this study, EFL students who lived in print-poor environments were given access to sets of sixty high-interest books, which were placed in classrooms, with another sixty made available in sets of six identical titles. The books were used for read alouds by the teacher, shared reading, and silent reading. Table 4–4 presents data from different provinces; in every case the readers outperformed those in comparison classes, and the gap widened with each year of reading.

Table 4–4
In-School Reading in South Africa

READING TEST SCORES

Province	Std 3		Std 4		Std 5	
	READ	NON-READ	READ	NON-READ	READ	NON-READ
Eastern Cape	32.5	25.6	44.0	32.5	58.1	39.0
Western Cape	36.2	30.2	40.4	34.3	53.0	40.4
Free State	32.3	30.1	44.3	37.1	47.2	40.5
Natal	39.5	28.3	47.0	32.3	63.1	35.1

PERCENT OF WRITTEN SENTENCES RATED AS FLUENT

Province	Std 3		Std 4		Std 5	
	READ	NON-READ	READ	NON-READ	READ	NON-READ
Eastern Cape	18.8	6.3	27.5	8.1	42.4	14.6
Western Cape	16.6	1.7	22.4	12.5	32.4	14.7
Free State	11.3	1.6	17.3	5.9	21.0	11.5
Natal	22.9	5.6	36.7	9.9	44.7	9.9
Total	16.4	3.7	24.5	9.1	34.9	12.5

READ = access to high-interest books provided by READ Educational Trust

Source: Elley (1998)

Tsang (1996) compared the effect of reading, writing, and extra mathematics activities on the writing performance of 104 secondary school level EFL students in Hong Kong. The reading group did self-selected reading (at home) from graded materials and wrote short reports "requiring minimal writing" on what they read (217). They were required to read eight books during the twenty-four-week study. The writing group wrote eight essays in the twenty-four-weeks, which were "impressionistically graded, given brief positive comments" and returned (217). Control students had extra mathematics enrichment.

Tsang reported that only the reading group made significant gains on essays evaluated for "overall impression" (Table 4–5) in ratings of content and language use (e.g., agreement, tense, number, word order). The writing group did not make significant gains in any area, and the controls got significantly worse in language use. There were no differences in other areas (vocabulary, organization, and mechanics). While these results confirm the power of reading, they are surprising considering the modest amount of reading done and the short duration of the study.

Mason (Mason and Krashen 1997) developed a version of sustained silent reading for university EFL students in Japan, termed "extensive reading," in which students do self-selected reading of pedagogical readers as well as easy authentic reading. In contrast with sustained silent reading, a minimal amount of accountability is required (e.g., a short summary of what was

Table 4–5
Gains in Essay Writing After Twenty-Four Weeks

GROUP	PRE	POST
Reading	61.77 (8.4)	68.3 (5.1)
Writing	62.69 (8.9)	68.3 (5.1)
Control	61.89 (9.5)	67.4 (5.8)

standard deviations in parentheses

Source: Tsang (1996)

read). In three separate studies, Mason found that extensive readers made greater gains than comparison students who participated in traditional form-based EFL classes.

Mason's first study is especially interesting. Her subjects were members of an experimental class for students who had failed previous EFL classes, termed a Sai Rishu (retakers) class. Seeing that the traditional curriculum was not working, Mason substituted extensive reading with graded readers. At the beginning of the semester, the experimental class was far behind the comparison class of regular students, but by the end of the semester they had nearly caught up in reading comprehension, and their adjusted mean score was significantly higher. Experimentals also showed a clear improvement in attitude toward English class.

There is considerable additional evidence for the "Reading Hypothesis" (Goodman 1982; Smith 1994) and it is consistent with a more general hypothesis: We acquire language through comprehension. Language acquisition takes place when we understand what we hear or what we read, the message.

Encouraging Free Reading

If free reading is valuable, how do we encourage it? Here again, research is consistent: Children read more when they have access to interesting reading material. Here is an example that strongly suggests that providing access results in more reading, which in turn results in superior progress in literacy development.

Rucker (1982) provided junior high school students with two free magazine subscriptions related to their interests. A "rural-remedial" group received the subscriptions for one and a half years and a "suburban" group received subscriptions for one year. Rucker reported that both magazine reading groups gained an additional one-half year on the CTBS Reading test over comparison groups (pretests and posttests given two years apart). There were no differences, however, on the CTBS Language test (mechanics, spelling).

A reasonable interpretation of these results is that the magazines not only served as a source of comprehensible text, but also stimulated more reading. As Rucker points out, magazines are probably the most "reader interest specific" of all mass media, and "may consequently be the most valuable as stimuli to reading" (33).

Light reading, in the form of magazines and comic books, is certainly not sufficient for the development of higher levels of literacy, but it is an important link that is missing from the lives of many students for financial reasons and because of disapproval of lighter texts on the part of some parents and librarians (Worthy 1996; Nell 1988). There is evidence that light reading serves as a conduit to heavier reading: Ujiie and Krashen (1996) studied comic book reading among middle school boys and found that those boys who described themselves as heavy comic book readers said they like to read more than lighter comic book readers and read more for pleasure. Those who did not read comic books reported less book reading than comic book readers. The view that comics can be a conduit to other reading is supported by studies showing that comic book texts contain more rare words than ordinary conversation does (Hayes and Ahrens 1988),[1] as well as case histories of readers who credit comic books with providing them with the linguistic basis for reading more difficult texts (e.g., Mathabane 1986).

Libraries

Simply providing access is the first and most important step in encouraging literacy development. Studies also show that children read more when they have a quiet, comfortable place to read. One place where both of these conditions (access and comfort and quiet) are met is the school library.

Two kinds of evidence confirm the importance of the

school library. First, children get a substantial percentage of their reading material from libraries (Table 4–6). When asked where they get their books to read, the range of children mentioning some kind of library is from 30 percent to 97 percent.

A second kind of evidence is a series of recent studies showing that better libraries are related to better reading, as measured by standardized tests of reading comprehension.

Lance (1994) found that money invested in the school library resulted in better library collections, which in turn resulted in superior reading achievement scores among elementary schools in Colorado. Lance controlled for a number of other factors, including the number of at-risk students at the school, which had a negative impact on reading achievement.

Krashen (1995) was an analysis of predictors of the NAEP fourth-grade reading test scores for forty-one states. The results of this analysis should be of great interest to Californians, because it

Table 4–6
Sources of Books for Eleven-Year-Old Children

STUDY	PERCENT WHO SAID THEY GOT THEIR BOOKS FROM LIBRARIES
Gaver 1963	30% to 63%
Lamme 1976	81%
Ingham 1981	72% to 97%
Swanton 1984	70%
Doig and Blackmore 1995	school library = 63%
	classroom library = 25%
	public library = 57%

was California's low performance on this test relative to other states that inspired the formation of a reading task force and the perception that something was very wrong with how reading was being taught in California. Among the best predictors of the NAEP performance was the number of books per student in the school library. McQuillan (1998) found similar results and expanded the analysis, demonstrating that access to print in general was a powerful predictor of NAEP scores. Time devoted to phonics instruction was a negative predictor: More time for phonics meant lower NAEP scores. When this effect of poverty was controlled, McQuillan found no relationship between phonics instruction and NAEP scores. Access to books was a significant predictor of reading achievement even when poverty was controlled, however, which strongly suggested that access to books is the crucial factor.

Access to books is also a significant predictor of SAT scores. McQuillan (1998) reported that a state's school library holdings as well as per capita public library circulation were independent and significant predictors of SAT scores for students in fifty states and the District of Columbia, controlling for school expenditures, computers, and teacher-student ratio.

Elley (1992) surveyed reading achievement in thirty-two countries and found that the quality of a country's school libraries was a significant predictor of its rank in reading. Not surprisingly, Elley reported that children in more economically developed countries read much better than those in less economically developed countries. This is, most likely, because children in wealthier countries have more access to print. Of special interest to us, however, Elley also found that children in the less wealthy countries with the best school libraries made up a large percentage of the gap (Table 4–7). The school library can make a profound difference.

Table 4–7

Mean Achievement by School Library Size: Fourteen-Year-Olds

	LOWEST QUARTER	2ND	3RD	HIGHEST QUARTER
Wealthy countries	521	525	536	535
Less wealthy countries	445	452	454	474
(mean = 500)				

Source: Elley (1992)

California

The poor performance of California's fourth graders on the NAEP reading examination has received a great deal of national publicity. California is far behind the national average in number of books per student in school libraries (Table 4–8), a result that is not a surprise given the strong correlation between books per student in libraries and scores on tests of reading achievement and California's poor performance on the NAEP.

Tables 4–9 and 4–10 show that California spends much less than the rest of the country does on school libraries and has far fewer librarians per pupil. California, in fact, ranks dead last in the United States in school librarians per pupil, far behind the second worst, Mississippi: California has one school librarian for every 6,248 students, while Mississippi has one for every 2,618. The national average is one school librarian for every 905 students (Sadowski and Meyer 1994). Moore (1993) has pointed out that inmates at the Preston Penal Institution have more access to books than California's high school students do, and the Preston library has one librarian for 815 inmates.

Table 4–8
Print Deprivation in California

BOOKS PER STUDENT

	Elementary school	Middle school	High school
USA	18 to 1	16 to 1	15 to 1
CA	13 to 1	11 to 1	8 to 1

Source: White (1990)

California's public libraries are not a big help: They now rank in the bottom seven of the country (Krashen 1996); they have experienced severe budget cuts in the last decade; and public library access has been drastically reduced. Public library budgets have been cut 25 percent since 1989 and public library hours have been cut 30 percent since 1987, and children's collections have been hit the hardest (McQuillan 1998). Children in California are clearly in a state of extreme print deprivation (pun intended).

Table 4–9
Money Spent on the School Library per Pupil

	ELEMENTARY SCHOOL	MIDDLE SCHOOL	HIGH SCHOOL
USA	$15.44	$15.50	$19.22
CA	$8.48	$7.48	$8.21

(Preston Penal Institution: $18.20)

Source: White (1990); Moore (1993)

Table 4–10
Number of Students per School Librarian

USA	906 to 1
CA	6,248 to 1

(Preston Penal Institution: 815 to 1)

Source: Sadowski and Meyer (1994); Moore (1993)

How the Print-Rich Get Richer

Data presented in Table 4–11 shows the amazing differences in print environments in different areas; in the sample studied by Smith, Constantino, and Krasnen (1996), the average child in Beverly Hills has more age-appropriate books at home than the average child in Watts and Compton has in his or her classroom library! Privileged children also have far better school libraries, public libraries (see Table 4–12, a comparison between Beverly Hills and working-class Santa Fe Springs), and have more access to bookstores.

The disparity extends to library services. Students in high-achieving schools in affluent areas are able to visit the school library more frequently, both independently and as a

Table 4–11
Print Environment in Three Communities

	BOOK-STORES	BOOKS IN HOME	CLASSROOM	LIBRARIES: SCHOOL	PUBLIC
Beverly Hills	5	199	392	60,000	200,600
Watts	0	.4	54	23,000	110,000
Compton	1	2.7	47	16,000	90,000

Source: Smith, Constantino, and Krashen (1996)

Table 4–12
Public Libraries in Two Communities

NUMBER OF:	BOOKS	CHILDREN'S MAGS	PROGRAMS	STAFF (CHILDREN'S SECTION)	POPULATION
Beverly Hills	60,000	30	12	14	32,000
Santa Fe Springs	13,000	20	3	0	16,000

children's magazines in SF Springs not kept in children's section of library

Source: Di Loreto and Tse (in press)

class, and are more likely to be allowed to take books home (Table 4–13). School is clearly not closing the gap—it is making things worse.

Allington et al. (1995) have reported similar findings for school libraries in New York State, reporting that of the twelve school libraries they studied, the six that served few poor children had more books than the six that served many poor children. What is especially noteworthy about their report is that the number of books per child in the schools serving poor children was 15.4, well above the average for the state of California. What is unacceptable elsewhere is above average in California.

In agreement with Smith, Constantino, and Krashen (Table 4–11), this study also found that classroom libraries in schools serving poorer children had fewer books, and in agreement with LeMoine et al. (1997) (Table 4–13), the study reported that

> in the schools serving many poor children access to the library was usually restricted to a single weekly visit. Several schools

Table 4–13
Print Access in Urban and Suburban Schools

	1 VISIT PER WEEK TO SCHOOL LIBRARY	INDEPENDENT VISITS	TAKE BOOKS HOME
High-achieving schools (urban) $n = 15$	100%	87%	73%
High-achieving schools (suburban) $n = 8$	100%	86%	100%
Low-achieving schools (urban) $n = 15$	60%	53%	47%

Source: LeMoine et al. (1997)

> also restricted the number of titles that children could borrow (usually one or two per visit). Two schools barred children from taking library books out of the building! No low-poverty school had such a restriction, and it was more common in these buildings for children to have relatively open access to the library throughout the day and, in some cases, before and after the regular classroom schedule. (24)

Note that seven out of the fifteen low-achieving California schools studied by LeMoine et al. did not allow children to take books home.

Libraries and Second Language Acquirers

The library situation is even worse for those acquiring English as a second language. Developing literacy in the primary language is an extremely efficient means of developing literacy in the second language (Cummins 1981). In order to become good readers in the primary language, however, children need to read in the primary language. The average Spanish-speaking family with limited English proficient children in school in the United States has only twenty-two books in their home (this figure refers to total books, not age-appropriate books for children) (Ramirez et al. 1991). Once again, school does not solve the problem: In the bilingual schools studied by Pucci (1994), school libraries had approximately one book per child in Spanish.

Constantino (1994) has reported that ESL students often have little idea of what the school library can offer, and that parents of ESL students were also nearly completely unaware of what was in libraries and how they operated (Constantino 1995).

Money for Libraries: Who is Paying Now?

Allington et al. (1995) reported that in their survey of schools in New York, "classrooms with the largest collections of trade books were those where teachers reported they purchased most of the books" (23–24). A great many teachers supply their students with books from their own funds. Guice et al. (1996) reported that 40 percent of the teachers they interviewed in six economically disadvantaged areas said that they purchased most of the books in their classroom collections themselves. Teachers who do this are in an impossible ethical dilemma; if they do not buy books for their students, there is nothing to read. If they do, and students progress in literacy, the basal series and unused software gets the credit. There is only one solution to this intolerable situation: a much greater investment by the school in books.

The money is there. A fraction of the investment we are willing to make for technology will provide access to good reading material for all children. Krashen (1996) shows that there is no convincing evidence that computers have ever helped anyone learn to read. A fraction of the investment we regularly make in testing will also provide access to good reading material for all children: Weighing the animal more precisely and more frequently will not help it grow faster—it needs to be fed.

My dream is a one-time investment, with the interest going to school and classroom libraries. Using California as an example, at the time of this writing, the governor is willing to invest a billion dollars for technology and training. At 5 percent interest, $1 billion would generate $10 per school child in California. If all of this money were invested in school libraries, this would increase California's investment from $8.50 per child, the current level, to $18.50 per child, just above the national average. And the money would be there forever.

Another advantage of a permanent fund is that schools would no longer have to compete against each other for tiny amounts, and the time now spent writing grants, evaluating grants, and searching for money could be utilized in more productive ways.

An Objection: If They Have Books, Will They Read Them?

If books are made available, will children read them? Two recent studies and several older studies strongly suggest that they will. Von Sprecken and Krashen (1998) observed eleven middle school classes during sustained silent reading time, during the middle of the school year: Overall, 90 percent of the children were reading.

In Ramos and Krashen (1998), second- and third-grade children who came from print-poor environments and who attended a school with a poor school library were taken to the public library monthly, during school time but before the library was open to the public. This allowed the children to explore the library, share books, and not be constrained by the need to remain quiet. Each child was allowed to take out ten books, which suddenly produced a substantial classroom library for use during sustained silent reading time and for reading at home. Three weeks after the first visit to the library, both children and parents were surveyed (Table 4–14). It was clear that the children enjoyed their visit; most reported reading more, that reading was easier, and that they wanted to return to the library. Parents' responses were consistent with the childrens' responses and tended to show even more enthusiasm.

Of course, the implication of this study is not simply to use the public library. The solution must come from school. The school involved in this study was lucky to have a cooperative, well-supplied public library close to the school. Others are not so lucky.

Table 4–14
Reactions to Library Visit

CHILD SURVEY ($N = 93$)

First time visited the public library: 52%

Returned to the library since the visit: 62%

Reading more since the library visit: 75%

Feel reading is easier now: 82%

PARENT SURVEY ($N = 75$)

Children more interested in reading since visiting the library: 96%

Notice improvement in child's reading: 94%

Child spends more time with books: 94%

Would like the library visiting program to continue: 100%

Child has asked parent to take them to the library since the visit: 67%

Source: Ramos and Krashen (1998)

Several studies confirm that those who participate in SSR show more interest in reading later (Pfau 1967; Pilgreen and Krashen 1993). The most spectacular is Greaney and Clarke (1973): Sixth-grade boys who participated in an in-school free reading program for eight and a half months not only did more leisure reading while they were in the program but also were still reading more than comparison students six years later. Simply providing interesting books for children is a powerful incentive for reading—perhaps the most powerful incentive possible. This conclusion is consistent with research showing that extrinsic incentives for reading have not been successful in encouraging reading (McQuillan 1997), while improving access to books and giving children a quiet, comfortable place to read them have been successful. Unfortunately, this option, which seems to be the most obvious and straightforward, is often neglected.

Postscript: A Criticism and a Response

Brady and Moats (1998) have several disagreements with the position presented here and elsewhere (Krashen 1997). They agree that access to books is important, but feel that "teachers can do little about the number of books students have at home or the number of books that are read aloud to students before they got to school" (7). True enough. But teachers can do a great deal to ensure that books are available in school and that children are read to in school.

As part of their argument that access to reading is not as crucial as I say it is, Brady and Moats point out that in California, "49% of the college-educated parents . . . in whose homes books are more plentiful, also read below a basic level of proficiency"

(7). There is no question that those with more education tend to provide their children with a more print-rich environment (Ortiz 1986), and there is no question that reading scores in California are depressed for all levels of parental education. While parental education has been shown to predict reading scores (Ortiz 1986), access to reading material also predicts reading achievement, even when parental education is statistically controlled (Ortiz 1986, Rowe 1991), as well as vocabulary development (Payne, Whitehurst and Angell 1994). Reduced access to books impacts all groups, regardless of level of education.

Brady and Moats consider my conclusion (in Krashen 1998), that "disadvantaged children read less well primarily because they have far less access to print" to be "extreme" because evidence for access is "correlational," and because children of poverty have other disadvantages. But there is good evidence showing that the problem is, in fact, access to books and not just poverty. While poverty has been shown to predict reading scores, access to reading material predicts reading achievement, even when poverty is controlled (McQuillan 1998, using NAEP scores for fourth graders; see also Wilkinson 1998). For children of low poverty, those who live in more print-rich environments will show greater literacy development, as well as greater oral vocabulary (Payne, Whitehurst and Angell 1994).

In addition, evidence of the impact of free reading on reading proficiency does not come only from correlational studies: For a review of the many experimental studies comparing groups who do different amounts of reading, see the text of this chapter, Chapter 3 of this book, and Krashen (1993).

Finally, Brady and Moats characterize my position inaccurately:

> In Krashen's view, reading is caught, not taught; kids learn it by doing it, and direct teaching of reading skills is unnecessary. . . .

Table 4–15

1994 Average Scores on the NAEP Grade 4 Reading Examination
by Parental Education Level

STATE	GRADUATED COLLEGE	SOME COLLEGE	HIGH SCHOOL GRADUATE	NOT HS GRADUATE
Massachusetts	232	230	212	206
Arizona	218	219	200	189
Florida	212	219	195	187
California	207	207	191	166
USA	222	222	206	188

Source: Campbell et al. (1996)

> In Krashen's ideal world, reading teachers would be librari-
> ans skilled at procuring books, promoting independent read-
> ing, and leading discussions. It would be unnecessary for
> them to understand the cognitive or linguistic precursors of
> successful reading, unnecessary for them to understand how
> print represents speech, and unnecessary for them to teach
> children how to read if they did not already know. School
> budgets would allow for hundreds of titles per classroom,
> and, faced with a poor reader, the teacher would assess the
> child's interests and hand him a list of good "leveled" books
> to read, assuming that what the child needed most was more
> practice. . . . Teacher preparation in reading would be lim-
> ited to courses on children's literature, classroom manage-
> ment, and resource allocation. (6)

This odd characterization has some truth. I certainly think that
reading teachers should work to provide a print-rich environ-

ment, and I think that school budgets should indeed allow for hundreds of titles per classroom. But Brady and Moat's description misses the main point of my position, as well as that of Smith (1994) and Goodman (1982): We acquire language and develop literacy when we understand the message, when we get comprehensible input. Handing children books does not guarantee comprehension. As noted earlier, the teacher's job in reading instruction is to provide interesting texts and help make these texts comprehensible. This can be done by providing discussion and background information (what McQuillan 1998 terms "elaborate assistance") and can also be done by providing direct instruction in linguistic form (what McQuillan 1998 calls "meta-linguistic assistance"). I have argued, as have others, that meta-linguistic assistance is quite limited (Krashen 1982, 1996). It is not, however, useless.

Note

1. According to Hayes and Ahrens (1988), it is highly unlikely that much educated vocabulary comes from conversation or television. They found that the frequency of less-common words in ordinary conversation, whether adult-to-child or adult-to-adult, was much lower than in even the "lightest" reading. About 95 percent of the words used in conversation and television are from the most frequent five thousand. Printed texts include far more uncommon words, leading Hayes and Ahrens to the conclusion that the development of lexical knowledge beyond basic words "requires literacy and extensive reading across a broad range of subjects" (409). Table 4–16 presents some of their data, including two of the three measures they used for word frequency. Note that light reading (comics, novels, other adult books, and magazines), although somewhat closer to conversation, occupies a position between conversation and abstracts of scientific papers. Clearly, light reading prepares the way for heavier reading.

Table 4–16

Common and Uncommon Words in Speech and Writing

	FREQUENT WORDS	RARE WORDS
Adults talking to children	95.6	9.9
Adults talking to adults (college grads)	93.9	17.3
Prime-time TV: adult	94.0	22.7
Children's books	92.3	30.9
Comic books	88.6	53.5
Books	88.4	52.7
Popular magazines	85.0	65.7
Newspapers	84.3	68.3
Abstracts of scientific papers	70.3	128.2

frequent words = percentage of text from most frequent 1,000 words
rare words = number of rare words (not in most common 10,000) per 1,000 tokens

Source: Hayes and Ahrens (1988)

References

Allen, L., J. Cipielewski, and K. Stanovich. 1992. "Multiple Indicators of Children's Reading Habits and Attitudes: Construct Validity and Cognitive Correlates." *Journal of Educational Psychology* 84: 489–503.

Allington, R., S. Guice, K. Baker, N. Michaelson, and S. Li. 1995. "Access to Books: Variations in Schools and Classrooms." *The Language and Literacy Spectrum* 5: 23–25.

Anderson, R., P. Wilson, and L. Fielding. 1988. "Growth in Reading and

How Children Spend Their Time Outside of School." *Reading Research Quarterly* 23: 285–303.

Brady, S., and L. Moats. 1998. "Buy Books, Teach Reading." *California Reader* 31 (4):6–10.

Campbell, J., P. Donahue, C. Reese, and G. Phillips. 1996. *NAEP 1994 Reading Report Card for the Nation and the States.* Washington, DC: Office of Educational Research and Improvement, US Dept of Education.

Cho, K. S., and S. Krashen. 1994. "Acquisition of Vocabulary from the Sweet Valley Kids Series: Adult ESL Acquisition." *Journal of Reading* 37: 662–667.

———. 1995a. "Becoming a Dragon: Progress in English as a Second Language Through Narrow Free Voluntary Reading." *California Reader* 29: 9–10.

———. 1995b. "From Sweet Valley Kids to Harlequins in One Year." *California English* 1 (1): 18–19.

Cohen, Y. 1997. "How Reading Got Me into Trouble." Class paper, Trenton State University.

Constantino, R. 1994. "Immigrant ESL High School Students' Understanding and Use of the School and Public Library." *SCOPE Journal* 93: 6–18.

———. 1995. "Minority Use of the Library." *California Reader* 28: 10–12.

Constantino, R., S. Y. Lee, K. S. Cho, and S. Krashen. 1997. "Free Voluntary Reading as a Predictor of TOEFL Scores." *Applied Language Learning* 8: 111–118.

Cummins, J. 1981. "The Role of Primary Language Developing in Promoting Success for Language Minority Students." In *Schooling and Language Minority Children: A Theoretical Framework,* ed. Office of Bilingual Bicultural Education, 3–49. Los Angeles: Evaluation, Dissemination and Assessment Center, California State University.

Cunningham, A., and K. Stanovich. 1990. "Assessing Print Exposure and Orthographic Processing Skill in Children: A Quick Measure of Reading Experience." *Journal of Educational Psychology* 82: 733–740.

Di Loreto, L., and L. Tse. In press. "Seeing is Believing: Disparity of Books in Two Los Angeles Area Public Libraries." *Public Library Quarterly.*

Doig, D., and A. Blackmore. 1995. "Leisure Reading: Attitudes and Practices of Australian Year 6 Children." *Australian Journal of Language and Literacy* 18: 204–217.

Elley, W. 1991. "Acquiring Literacy in a Second Language: The Effect of Book-Based Programs." *Language Learning* 41 (3): 375–411.

———. 1992. *How in the World Do Children Read?* Hamburg, Germany: International Association for the Evaluation of Educational Achievement.

———. 1998. *Raising Literacy Levels in Third World Countries: A Method That Works.* Culver City, CA: Language Education Associates.

Elley, W., and F. Mangubhai. 1983. "The Impact of Reading on Second Language Learning." *Reading Research Quarterly* 19: 53–67.

Fader, D. 1976. *The New Hooked on Books.* New York: Berkeley Books.

Gaver, M. 1963. *Effectiveness of Centralized Library Service in Elementary Schools.* New Brunswick, NJ: Rutgers University Press.

Goodman, K. 1982. *Language, Literacy, and Learning.* London: Routledge Kegan Paul.

Greaney, V., and M. Clarke. 1973. "A Longitudinal Study of the Effects of Two Reading Methods on Leisure-Time Reading Habits." In *Reading: What of the Future?* ed. D. Moyle, 107–114. London: United Kingdom Reading Association.

Guice, S., R. Allington, P. Johnston, K. Baker, and N. Michaelson. 1996. "Access? Books, Children, and Literature-Based Curriculum in Schools." *The New Advocate* 9 (3): 197–207.

Hayes, D., and M. Ahrens. 1988. "Vocabulary Simplification for Children: A Special Case of 'Motherese'?" *Journal of Child Language* 15: 395–410.

Ingham, J. 1981. *Books and Reading Development: The Bradford Book Flood Experiment.* London: Heinemann Educational Books.

Kim, H., and S. Krashen. In press. "The Author Recognition and Magazine Recognition Tests, and Free Voluntary Reading as Predictors of Vocabulary Development in English as a Foreign Language." *System*.

Krashen, S. 1982. *Principles and Practice in Second Language Acquisition*. New York: Prentice Hall.

———. 1993. *The Power of Reading*. Englewood, CO: Libraries Unlimited.

———. 1995. "School Libraries, Public Libraries, and the NAEP Reading Scores." *School Library Media Quarterly* 23: 235–238.

———. 1996. *Every Person a Reader*. Culver City, CA: Language Education Associates.

———. 1997. "Some Problems with 'Informed Instruction for Reading Success: Foundations for Teacher Preparation.' " *California Reader* 31 (2): 6–12.

Lamme, L. 1976. "Are Reading Habits and Abilities Related?" *Reading Teacher* 30: 21–27.

Lance, K. 1994. "The Impact of School Library Media Centers on Academic Achievement." In *School Library Media Annual*, vol. 12, ed. C. Kuhlthau, 188–197. Englewood, CO: Libraries Unlimited.

Lee, S. Y., and S. Krashen. 1996. "Free Voluntary Reading and Writing Competence in Taiwanese High School Students." *Perceptual and Motor Skills* 83: 687–690.

Lee, S. Y., S. Krashen, and L. Tse. 1997. "The Author Recognition Test and Vocabulary Knowledge: A Replication." *Perceptual and Motor Skills* 85: 1428–1430.

Lee, Y. O., S. Krashen, and B. Gribbons. 1996. "The Effect of Reading on the Acquisition of English Relative Clauses." *ITL: Review of Applied Linguistics* 113–114: 263–273.

LeMoine, N., E. Brandlin, B. O'Brian, and J. McQuillan. 1997. "The (Print)-Rich Get Richer: Library Access in Low- and High-Achieving Elementary Schools." *California Reader* 30: 23–25.

Mangubhai, F., and W. Elley. 1982. "The Role of Reading in Promoting ESL." *Language Learning and Communication* 1: 151–60.

Mason, B., and S. Krashen. 1997. "Extensive Reading in English as a Foreign Language." *System* 25: 91–102.

Mathabane, M. 1986. *Kaffir Boy*. New York: Plume.

McQuillan, J. 1996. "New Questions Amidst the Aftershocks: What Caused California's Reading Crisis?" *California English* 1 (4): 10.

———. 1997. "The Effects of Incentives on Reading." *Reading Research and Instruction* 36: 111–125.

———. 1998. *The Literacy Crisis: False Claims and Real Solutions.* Portsmouth, NH: Heinemann.

Moore, R. 1993. "California Dreamin'." *Emergency Librarian* 21:17.

Nell, V. 1988. *Lost in a Book*. New Haven: Yale University Press.

Ortiz, V. 1986. "Reading Activities and Reading Proficiency Among Hispanic, Black, and White Students." *American Journal of Education* 95: 58–76.

Payne, A., G. Whitehurst, and A. Angell. 1994. "The Role of Home Literacy Environment in the Development of Language Ability in Preschool Children from Low-Income Families." *Early Childhood Research Quarterly* 9: 427–440.

Pfau, D. 1967. "Effects of Planned Recreational Reading Programs." *Reading Teacher* 21: 34–39.

Pilgreen, J., and S. Krashen. 1993. "Sustained Silent Reading with English as a Second Language High School Students: Impact on Reading Comprehension, Reading Frequency, and Reading Enjoyment." *School Library Media Quarterly* 22: 21–23.

Pucci, S. 1994. "Supporting Spanish Language Literacy: Latino Children and Free Reading Resources in the Schools." *Bilingual Research Journal* 18: 67–82.

Ramirez, D., S. Yuen, D. Ramey, and D. Pasta. 1991. *Final Report: Longitudinal Study of Structured English Immersion Strategy, Early-Exit and Late-Exit Bilingual Education Programs for Language Minority Student,* vol. 1. San Mateo, CA: Aguirre International.

Ramos, F., and S. Krashen. 1998. "The Impact of One Trip to the Public Library: Making Books Available May Be the Best Incentive for Reading." *The Reading Teacher* 51 (7): 614–615.

Rodrigo, V., J. McQuillan, and S. Krashen. 1996. "Free Voluntary Reading and Vocabulary Knowledge in Native Speakers of Spanish." *Perceptual and Motor Skills* 83: 648–650.

Rowe, K. 1991. "The Influence of Reading Activity at Home on Students' Attitudes Toward Reading, Classroom Attentiveness and Reading Achievement: An Application of Structural Equation Modeling." *British Journal of Educational Psychology* 61: 19–35.

Rucker, B. 1982. "Magazines and Teenage Reading Skills: Two Controlled Field Experiments." *Journalism Quarterly* 59: 28–33.

Sadowski, M., and R. Meyer. 1994. "Staffing for Success." *School Library Journal* (June): 29–31.

Segal, J. 1997. "Summer Daze." Class paper, Trenton State University.

Smith, C., R. Constantino, and S. Krashen. 1996. "Differences in Print Environment for Children in Beverly Hills, Compton, and Watts." *Emergency Librarian* 24 (4): 8–9.

Smith, F. 1994. *Understanding Reading*. 5th ed. Hillsdale, NJ: Erlbaum.

Stanovich, K., and R. West. 1989. "Exposure to Print and Orthographic Processing." *Reading Research Quarterly* 24: 402–433.

Stanovich, K., R. West, and M. Harrison. 1995. "Knowledge Growth and Maintenance Across the Life Span: The Role of Print Exposure." *Developmental Psychology* 31: 811–826.

Stokes, J., S. Krashen, and J. Kartchner. In press. "Factors in the Acquisition of the Present Subjunctive in Spanish: The Role of Reading and Study." *ITL: Review of Applied Linguistics.*

Swanton, S. 1984. "Minds Alive: What and Why Gifted Students Read for Pleasure." *School Library Journal* 30: 99–102.

Tsang, W. K. 1996. "Comparing the Effects of Reading and Writing on Writing Performance." *Applied Linguistics* 17: 210–233.

Ujiie, J., and S. Krashen. 1996. "Comic Book Reading, Reading Achievement, and Pleasure Reading Among Middle Class and Chapter 1 Middle School Students." *Reading Improvement* 33: 50–54.

Von Sprecken, D., and S. Krashen. 1998. "Do Students Read During Sustained Silent Reading?" *California Reader* 32 (1): 11–13.

West, R., K. Stanovich, and H. Mitchell. 1993. "Reading in the Real World and Its Correlates." *Reading Research Quarterly* 28: 35–50.

White, H. 1990. "School Library Collections and Services: Ranking the States." *School Library Media Quarterly* 19: 13–26.

Wilkinson, I. 1998. "Dealing with Diversity: Achievement Gaps in Reading Literacy Among New Zealand Students." *Reading Research Quarterly* 33 (2): 144–167.

Worthy, J. 1996. "Removing Barriers to Voluntary Reading for Reluctant Readers: The Role of School and Classroom Libraries." *Language Arts* 73: 483–492.

5

Phonemic Awareness (PA) Training for Prelinguistic Children:
Do We Need Prenatal PA?

California's fourth graders ranked close to last in the country on the fourth-grade National Association for Educational Progress reading examination for the last two administrations. This dismal performance prompted the State of California to create a Reading Task Force, and the Task Force responded boldly to the crisis, urging that greater attention be paid to basics—such as phonemic awareness (PA, the ability to divide a word into its component sounds), phonics, spelling, and grammar—and urging that instruction in these areas begin early (California Department of Education 1995). Evaluation, they suggested, should begin in kindergarten, with screening for phonemic awareness, and intervention programs should begin no later than the middle of first grade (recommendations 2 and 3). The Task Force also recommended that phonemic awareness training should be "initiated in pre-kindergarten" (recommendation 6) and that intervention should be "rigorous" (recommendation 3).

This response appears to be a step in the right direction, but is it too little, too late? It has been established that poor readers in early school years often remain poor readers later on (Juel 1994), that three-year-old children differ in phonemic awareness (Chaney 1992), that phonemic awareness is a predictor of reading achievement, and that PA can be improved with training (Lundberg, Frost, and Peterson 1988; Cunningham 1990; Ball and Blachman 1991; Brady et al. 1994). Thus, it appears reasonable, and even imperative, that we begin phonemic awareness training much earlier. This suggestion is justified on academic as well as affective grounds: Without very early phonemic awareness training, some children will enter preschool behind their peers in phonemic awareness, which means difficulties with preschool phonemic awareness activities and certain failure at the kindergarten phonemic awareness screening. To avoid this problem, and the emotional scarring that would result from failing preschool, very early intervention is called for.

In pre-speech stages, we need pre-speech phonemic awareness. For children who have no or very little language development, we need to adapt regular phonemic awareness activities:

1. Yopp (1995) recommends the use of stories that contain language that stimulate phonemic awareness, such as stories in which certain sounds are emphasized. Because prelinguistic children will not understand such stories, we can focus just on the rhythm and syllable structure. Instead of "Once upon a time there were three bears . . ." the trainer can simply use a syllable such as /ba/: "ba ba ba ba ba, ba ba ba ba" (use intonation similar to the first line of "The Three Bears"). This will sensitize the child to the /b/ sound as well as to syllables and rhythm. Over time, more segmental phonemic awareness can be developed by altering the consonant and vowel, moving gradually to blends.

2. The previous activity can be generalized. To sensitize the child to simple consonant-vowel combinations, trainers can focus on one combination each day. On Monday, for example, all utterances to the child will be /ba/ and only /ba/. Instead of "give me a kiss," the caregiver would say, "ba ba ba ba," making the appropriate gestures with the appropriate intonation. On Tuesday, the focus would be /da/. Over a period of several months, all possible consonant-vowel combinations can be covered, and more complex syllables can be used.

3. Yopp recommends segmentation activities, such as the use of songs in which sounds are repeated: "For instance, when singing 'Pop goes the weasel,' the teacher may encourage the children to sing 'P-p-p-POP goes the weasel!' for the final line in the song" (1992, 701). This is a splendid activity, but it can be expanded to deliberate stuttering all day long. Caregivers can emphasize initial consonants this way.

Even Earlier Intervention

If this intervention fails, and we find children failing the preschool phonemic awareness test, we should, of course, consider even earlier intervention. Studies have shown that newborns can discriminate consonants. If a brief segment of speech is played for newborns sucking on a nipple for milk, sucking rate will increase (Eimas et al. 1971). The study took advantage of this phenomena to show that newborns have the perceptual underpinnings of phonemic awareness. They played the syllable /ba/ when sufficient sucking was demonstrated. After a few minutes, however, the infants tired of /ba/ and sucking rate decreased. Eimas et al. found that sucking rate would increase again if the syllable was changed. Using this technique, they demonstrated that even one-month-old babies could distinguish the phonemes /b/ and /p/.

The implications of this discovery for literacy development are obvious: universal screening for consonant discrimination at one month of age, with training techniques for infants who perform significantly below their peers.

Prenatal Phonemic Awareness

Even infant phonemic awareness training may not be enough. There is now evidence from twin studies that phonemic awareness may be inherited (Olson et al. 1989). Those born with deficient phonemic awareness will be at a clear disadvantage when tested just after birth. To make sure these PA-poor babies have a chance to compete with their age-mates, we urgently need to encourage research in genetic engineering and prenatal phonemic awareness, along with eugenics: Couples considering marriage may want to have their prospective partner screened for defective phonemic awareness. (Of course, PA screening is only a crude measure: The PA gene might be recessive.)

Use of these procedures, of course, may have disadvantages. Use of syllables instead of real language, for example, may have detrimental effects on caregiver-child communication. This is, however, a small price to pay for the gains it will produce in phonemic awareness. A PA-trained child can enter preschool with confidence, knowing that he or she can actively participate in any phonemic awareness activity and be ready for the kindergarten screening exam.

Postscript: The Alternative

There is an alternative to intensive and early PA training. It has been established that PA develops on its own; young children become sensitive to rhyme at an early age (Goswami and Bryant

1990), and there is evidence that awareness of syllables develops early and without instruction (Wimmer et al. 1991; Morais et al. 1986), while the ability to segment phonemes appears to be a consequence of literacy development (Mann 1986; Read et al. 1986; Morais et al. 1986; Perfetti et al. 1987; Wimmer et al. 1991; Lie 1991). Juel's subjects (Juel 1994), in fact, all attained perfect scores on her test of phonemic awareness by grade three. Finally, control subjects in PA training studies (cited above) make clear progress in phonemic awareness without any special training.

There is also good reason to hypothesize that gaps in reading level are relatively easy to make up when children get to read interesting texts, when they get "hooked on books" (Fader 1976; Krashen 1993). Juel (1994) calculated that by grade four good readers had read 178,000 words in school, while poor readers had read only 80,000. Let us assume that good readers read much more at home, and that by grade four they have read over a million words, while poor readers read nothing at home. Thus, the difference between them is about a million words. It is not difficult to make up this gap: Comic books contain about 2000 words each; 50 comics thus contain about 100,000 words, about 10 percent of the gap. One Sweet Valley Kids novel contains about 7000 words; 14 of them contain 100,000, another 10 percent of the gap. As additional evidence that this is possible, McQuillan (1998) reported that home-schooled children who were allowed to begin to read whenever they wanted to occasionally began very late but rapidly achieved "grade level" and beyond, and Elley (1992), in a study of reading ability in thirty-two countries, reported "some advantage for an earlier start, but it can be said that countries which begin instruction in reading at age seven have largely caught up with the five- and six-year-old starters in reading ability by age nine" (37). Finland, with the best readers in the world, starts reading instruction at age seven. Also in support of this alternative, it has been shown that quality of school libraries is associated with achievement in reading comprehension (Elley 1992; Lance 1994; Krashen 1995; McQuillan 1998).

While free reading could easily close the gap by grade four or five, super-early PA training has definite advantages. First, it ensures grade-level performance by kindergarten and success on the screening exam. Second, free reading is pleasant; if allowed simply to read for pleasure, children might get the wrong idea of what school is about. Life is tough, and we need to prepare them for life. The California Task Force recommends phonemic awareness training from preschool all the way through to the eighth grade (California Department of Education 1995, 18–19): Children will be matching sounds of words (grades K through 3), blending phonemes (K through 8), doing segmentation exercises on initial and final phonemes (grade 1), working up to medial phonemes (grades 1 through 3), and doing "more complex segmenting, blending, and transposition" all the way to grade 8, a program far beyond the recommendations of the most devoted PA researchers (Ball and Blachman's subjects did a seven-week program, while Cunningham's did a ten-week program. Lundberg, Frost, and Peterson's went for a full year, but even this is less than what is proposed by the task force). While these abilities will emerge without special training, and although it is true that millions of people have learned to read perfectly well without PA training, this plan has the clear advantage of preventing children from taking the easy way out—that is, developing phonemic awareness by simply reading. This intense focus on the meaningless aspects of reading (along with the heavy focus on phonics) will provide excellent discipline and help introduce them to the idea that life is full of meaningless tasks.

Third, more reading means more money for libraries. California, last in the country in NAEP reading, is also near last in school libraries, in terms of books per students and number of school librarians per student. California, however, is so far behind in school libraries that catching up is nearly impossible without a massive commitment. We thus need to consider other avenues.[1]

Note

1. Moore (1993) offers a useful suggestion for students who want to read but don't have a good school library: "If you're fourteen and you really want to go to the library, your best bet is to steal a car, get high, rob a Seven Eleven, and shoot the clerk. That way, you'll be incarcerated by the California Youth Authority. They will provide an education, and a school library until you are released at twenty-five. One of their facilities serves 1750 youthful offenders with a full-time librarian and $50,000 for books. Use a gun—go to the library!" (17). In contrast, California has about six hundred full-time credentialed librarians for a school population of more than five million (Moore 1993).

References

Ball, E., and B. Blachman. 1991. "Does Phonemic Segmentation Training in Kindergarten Make a Difference in Early Word Recognition and Developmental Spelling?" *Reading Research Quarterly* 26: 49–66.

Brady, S., A. Fowler, B. Stone, and N. Winbury. 1994. "Training Phonological Awareness: A Study with Inner-City Kindergarten Children." *Annals of Dyslexia* 44: 26–59.

California Department of Education. 1995. *Every Child a Reader: The Report of the California Reading Task Force.* Sacramento, CA: California Department of Education.

Chaney, C. 1992. "Language Development, Metalinguistic Skills, and Print Awareness in 3-Year-Old Children." *Applied Psycholinguistics* 13: 485–514.

Cunningham, A. 1990. "Explicit Versus Implicit Instruction in Phonemic Awareness." *Journal of Experimental Child Psychology* 50: 429–444.

Eimas, P., E. Siquel and P. Jusczyk, and J. Vigorito. 1971. "Speech Perception in Infants." *Science* 171: 303–306.

Elley, W. 1992. *How in the World Do Children Read?* Hamburg, Germany: International Association for the Evaluation of Educational Achievement.

Fader, D. 1976. *The New Hooked on Books.* New York: Berkley Books.

Goswami, U., and P. Bryant. 1990. *Phonological Skills and Learning How to Read.* Hove, UK: Erlbaum.

Juel, C. 1994. *Learning to Read and Write in One Elementary School.* New York: Springer-Verlag.

Krashen, S. 1993. *The Power of Reading.* Englewood, NJ: Libraries Unlimited.

———. 1995. "School Libraries, Public Libraries, and NAEP Scores." *School Library Media Quarterly* 23: 235–237.

Krashen, S., and J. McQuillan. 1996. *The Case for Late Intervention: Once a Good Reader, Always a Good Reader.* Culver City, CA: Language Education Associates.

Lance, K. 1994. "The Impact of School Library Media Centers on Academic Achievement." In *School Library Media Annual,* vol. 12, ed. C. Kuhlthau, 188–197. Englewood, CO: Libraries Unlimited.

Lie, A. 1991. "Effects of a Training Program for Stimulating Skills in Word Analysis in First-Grade Children." *Reading Research Quarterly* 26: 234–250.

Lundberg, I., J. Frost, and O. Peterson. 1988. "Effects of an Extensive Program for Stimulating Phonological Awareness in Preschool Children." *Reading Research Quarterly* 23: 263–284.

Mann, V. 1986. "Phonological Awareness: The Role of Reading Experience." *Cognition* 24: 65–92.

McQuillan, J. 1998. *The Literacy Crisis: False Claims and Real Solutions.* Portsmouth, NH: Heinemann.

Moore, R. 1993. "California Dreamin'." *Emergency Librarian* 21: 17.

Morais, J., P. Bertelson, L. Cary, and J. Alegria. 1986. "Literacy Training and Speech Segmentation." *Cognition* 24: 45–64.

Olson, R., B. Wise, F. Conners, J. Rack, and D. Fulker. 1989. "Specific Deficits in Component Reading and Language Skills: Genetic and Environmental Influences." *Journal of Reading Disabilities* 22: 339–348.

Perfetti, C., I. Beck, L. Bell, and C. Hughes. 1987. "Phonemic Knowledge and Learning to Read Are Reciprocal: A Longitudinal Study of First Grade Children." *Merrill-Palmer Quarterly* 33: 283–319.

Read, C., Z. Yun-Fei, N. Hong-Yin, and D. Bao-Qing. 1986. "The Ability to Manipulate Speech Sounds Depends on Knowing Alphabetic Writing." *Cognition* 24: 31–44.

Wimmer, H., K. Landerl, R. Linortner, and P. Hummer. 1991. "The Relationship of Phonemic Awareness to Reading Acquisition: More Consequence than Precondition but Still Important." *Cognition* 40: 219–249.

Yopp, H. 1992. "Developing Phonemic Awareness in Young Children." *The Reading Teacher* 45: 696–703.

———. 1995. "Read-Aloud Books for Developing Phonemic Awareness: An Annotated Bibliography." *The Reading Teacher* 48: 538–542.

Index